D1570675

THE GOLDEN STRING

BY *David A. Redding*

The Parables He Told
Psalms of David
The Miracles of Christ
The New Immorality
If I Could Pray Again
The Couch and the Altar
The Faith of Our Fathers
Until You Bless Me
God Is Up to Something
Getting Through the Night
Lives He Touched
The Prayers I Love
Jesus Makes Me Laugh
What Is the Man
Flagler and His Church
Liberty Beginnings
Before You Call I Will Answer
Amazed by Grace
The Golden String

DAVID REDDING

THE GOLDEN STRING

FLEMING H. REVELL COMPANY
OLD TAPPAN, NEW JERSEY

Unless otherwise identified, Scripture quotations in this book are taken from the King James Version of the Bible.

Scripture quotations identified RSV are taken from the Revised Standard Version of the Bible, Copyrighted © 1946, 1952, 1971, by the Division of Christian Education of the National Council of the Churches of Christ in the United States of America, and are used by permission. All rights reserved.

Scripture quotations identified NKJV are taken from The New King James Version. Copyright © 1979, 1980, 1982 Thomas Nelson, Inc., Publishers.

Scripture quotations identified PHILLIPS are taken from THE NEW TESTAMENT IN MODERN ENGLISH, Revised Edition—J.B. Phillips, translator. © J.B. Phillips 1958, 1960, 1972. Used by permission of Macmillan Publishing Co., Inc.

Prayer by Betty Scott Stamm on page 136 is from *Let Me Be a Woman* by Elisabeth Elliot, © 1976. Used by permission of Tyndale House Publishers, Inc.

Library of Congress Cataloging-in-Publication Data

Redding, David A.
   The golden string.
   1. Christian life—1960–   . I. Title.
BV4501.2.R387   1988   284.4   87-32327
ISBN 0-8007-1570-5

Copyright © 1988 by David A. Redding
Published by the Fleming H. Revell Company
Old Tappan, New Jersey 07675
Printed in the United States of America

To Dee

Acknowledgments

Beth Dixon
Marion Telford Redding
Doris Woods Cary

Contents

Introduction: This Way Out   13

I. **THE STARTING BLOCK**

  1. *Surely There Was an Eden*   19

  2. *My Father's Servants Live Better*   29

  3. *The First Search for the Lost City*   37

  4. *The Practice Run to the Promised Land*   47

  5. *Follow Me*   59

  6. *Jesus' Most Famous Travel Tip*   71

  7. *Thy Word Is a Light Upon My Path*   83

II. **FORKS IN THE ROAD**

    8. *The Chief Obstacle*   *99*

    9. *No Package Deal*   *111*

   10. *Battling the Green Distraction*   *119*

   11. *Slipping Through the Needle's Eye*   *129*

   12. *Fighting Off the Death Wish*   *137*

III. **ALL THE WAY HOME**

   13. *The Path Through Despair You Have Provided Me*   *149*

   14. *To Keep You Company on the Way*   *161*

   15. *One Step at a Time*   *169*

   16. *The Father Will Run to Greet You Too*   *177*

I give you the end of a Golden String,
only wind it into a ball,
It will lead you in at heaven's gate
Built in Jerusalem's wall.

William Blake

Introduction
This
Way
Out

*H*ow do I get to heaven? How do you answer that question? "Be good," "Read your Bible," or console yourself with Saint Paul: "Whoever calls on the name of Jesus will be saved." The repentant thief who died on the Cross beside Jesus was a little late getting around to it when he finally said, "Lord, remember me when You come into Your Kingdom." Yet Jesus promptly replied, "Today you shall be with me in Paradise."

But how do we get to heaven? It is a longer journey for

most of us than for the thief, and the answer is a little different for each of us, because none of us starts at exactly the same place. However, there are God-given navigational aids hidden in Scripture and shining in the individual trips there that the faithful have made. This book highlights their journeys to guide the modern pilgrim to the Holy City.

A brilliant lawyer once dared to ask Jesus exactly how to find this heavenly home (Luke 10). Jesus was enthusiastic about the question, not only because the lawyer came up with what is regarded as Jesus' own unique commandment, but because the lawyer probed till he had drawn from Jesus His most famous story. That story of the Good Samaritan specifically illustrates how to be a good neighbor, but Jesus told it in the context of the lawyer's opening question: "How shall I inherit eternal life?" It was Jesus' most famous travel tip, as we call it in chapter 6, which is just one of the guidelines illumined to assist you in your own pilgrimage.

Going to heaven also means going home. In a sense, all humanity started out in heaven. Heaven, or Eden, is where we fell from. This book begins, as the Bible does, with Adam and Eve evacuating the perfect Garden of Eden. While heaven and Eden are not quite synonymous, we are told a heavenly Eden was once on earth and we still pray for it to come back again in the Lord's Prayer: "Thy Kingdom come on earth as it is in heaven."

While we cannot fully understand nor clearly explain, we're not really from earth, but exiled here, like the prodigal to a far country. Our future destination is also behind us somewhere, hidden in our beginnings. We belong, and long to return like the lost son, to our

Introduction
___

Heavenly Father. Can you imagine anything more marvelous? Our belief is that when you take your last breath at the end of the trail, you will see Him running toward you with outstretched arms to welcome you home.

How do we get to heaven? This book attempts to splice together the various strands of directions along which we have to wind our way. It is as though we do have a "Golden String," as Blake spoke of in his poem "Jerusalem," to guide us through our dark maze into the place of eternal light:

> I give you the end of a Golden String,
> only wind it into a ball,
> It will lead you in at Heaven's gate
> Built in Jerusalem's wall.

David A. Redding
Sky Farm

PART I

THE
STARTING
BLOCK

1

Surely There Was an Eden

Once upon a time there was an enchanted Garden. The Bible, which is our starting block, calls it *Eden*. The first man and woman lived there with perfect peace in their deepest hearts. Life was no trouble at all, which did not mean it was dull. Life was a ball, where no midnight ever turned a princess's carriage back into a pumpkin. Life was a picnic without ants or mosquitoes, so no one got bitten or mad or sick. God was as plain as day, so no one ever died. Adam and Eve not only had each other, they had everything. It was heaven on earth.

However, for years now scientists and seminarians have been so busy reminding us that the story of the Garden of Eden is only a story, that most of us tossed it into the attic of our faith long ago. So you won't find it in our history books anymore; at best it is regarded as a noble specimen of ancient tribal lore. As the story works out, Adam not only left the Garden, he fell into thinking that the Garden never was, as though the serpent made him eat his memory along with the apple.

I have been properly credentialed with all these scholarly reservations and was once to blame for spreading this contagious condescension regarding the Bible, having been bitten by the same questions that incensed Religion 101. I have now lost confidence in such academic arrogance, for that can be as absurd as the smug assumptions of the most rabid literalist.

Whatever the Garden of Eden story is, it introduces the Word of God. Bewildering as the story is, it existed before and will last long after the famous last words of our most sophisticated authorities are forgotten. Long after our brilliant commentaries have been buried and our miles of microfilm have been pulverized in the dust, this story of creation will continue to penetrate to the marrow of our bones. And even when we see God face to face, as Paul promises in First Corinthians, and we finally hear His last word on how it all began, His answer will hardly improve upon the revelation that already plumbs us so powerfully in Genesis One.

I never expected to hear it from a celebrated philologist of Oxford University in England, but J. R. R. Tolkien sent me flying back to the story of the Garden again. Aware of the longing that lies inexplicably in all our hearts, he wrote of this yearning in a letter to his son, Christopher:

. . . but certainly there was an Eden on this very unhappy earth. We all long for it, and we are constantly glimpsing it; our whole nature at its best and least corrupted, its gentlest and most humane, is still soaked with the sense of exile.

Because this learned professor, who has charmed the world with such fantasies as *The Hobbit* and *The Fellowship of the Ring*, said this to his son, I am persuaded to a new respect for Eden as our former estate. I confess I do not fully understand, nor has anyone ever been able to explain it to me, but our contemporary suffering is due to homesickness for a lost world. It represents our struggle against despair for its return.

Rediscovering the Garden of Eden is not an easy assignment for the twentieth century. It is more elusive than the proverbial needle in the haystack. We live in a universe so vast that if the thickness of this sheet of paper signifies the distance from earth to the moon, the sun is seventy feet away, and the edge of the universe an incredible number of miles. No casual archaeologist would be able to pinpoint this phantom Garden in such an endless sea of space.

Earth has become a far country where we have awakened after a prodigal ride in space. And we are as mystified by our arrival as though we'd been blindfolded all the way here. We can scarcely see now, although it is quite obvious that we are somehow "away."

We can also tell that we can't stay here. This place will burn down or dry up, even before we're blown away. Everything about earth shouts impermanence. We are like mariners marooned on a sinking solar island. Earth is a lost ball. We must get out of here—or go out and come in all over again.

How do we find our way back to where we belong?

Earth's our only clue. It is not only a planet, it is also a parable that gives away our position. Earth is a navigational aid to assist us in rediscovering our primary source.

Life here in the dust is like a dream. The meaning is not transparent, but it is decipherable. As in interpreting a dream, we must read between the lines. The way the sun comes up says something. Jesus came up with about forty stories from scenes that are familiar to earthlings and are also highly suggestive of where we go from here. For instance: "The kingdom of heaven is like leaven, which a woman took and hid in three measures of meal till it was all leavened" (Matthew 13:33 NKJV).

Earth's not an end in itself. It is a murky window of eternity. We must look through it the best we can. So earth is a sacrament, which is, as Augustine defined: "A visible sign of an invisible grace." John Milton made that memorable in his verse:

> What if earth be but a shadow of heaven and things
> therein each to the other like more than on earth
> is thought.

Even our fairy tales and myths reverberate with our desire for a journey back from this foreign territory. Abandoned Hansel and Gretel dropped grains of corn, so they could retrace their steps. In *The Wizard of Oz*, Dorothy followed the yellow brick road. Perhaps the most arresting Greek antecedent of this recurring theme was on Minos where each year a youth would be sacrificed to a Minotaur in an inextricable labyrinth until one maiden handed her lover, who had been selected for this deadly favor, a piece of string. She held the other end, so he could wind his way back, which is reminiscent of Odysseus' return in Homer.

Scripture, too, offers the most haunting imagery about our emergency exit. Rahab, the prostitute of Jericho, extended the scarlet line so Joshua's spies could be lowered to safety on solid ground outside the wall of the enemy city. Wise men from the East followed a star. Moses led the Israelites in the wilderness by a pillar of cloud by day and a pillar of fire by night. Just as Tolkien's Bilbo in *The Hobbit* journeys to a rendezvous with destiny, so the Bible presents God's Word as "a light unto our path, and a lamp unto our feet." William Blake incorporated it all for us in his magnificent poetic image that entitles this book and serves as our chief metaphor.

> *I give you the end of a Golden String,*
> *only wind it into a ball,*
> *It will lead you in at heaven's gate*
> *Built in Jerusalem's wall.*

Sophomores may throw out the Garden of Eden upon the slightest encouragement from agnostic faculty, along with associated positives such as the Golden String. Then we are shocked when these "enlightened" youths show such a predilection for weird cults, falling for animal sacrifices as though the future could be found and read in the liver of a chicken, as back in ancient Babylon. Why not choose "the end of a Golden String"?

Our globe is cracked down the middle by a curtain of iron. We see smoke wherever we look, much of it because our news media have a nose for the market of conflict. They've already sold us a strong dose of it in the morning as soon as we get up and last thing at night before we go to bed. It all reminds us, though, of a fairer retirement than Florida, a more memorable trip than Hawaii; our hearts are restless for "home where I belong."

"I give you the end of a Golden String." It is not instant gratification, as though we were boarding some spiritual space shuttle. It is a walk. We start at the beginning—the most difficult place. A person cannot find the end of the Golden String until he comes to the end of *his* string.

No one ever wants God's help, no one ever wants out, until he's down and out. While the going's good, he'll go on the same old way. Alcoholics Anonymous won't pester a drunk with their program until a penitent "has had it" on his own. Until a drunk has crashed hard, he's not ready to let go of his rope and try God's.

None of us is any different. We are like the prodigal who stayed in the far country until he was starved out. An easy transfer into Christianity is "easy come, easy go." This is the game with God that churches typically sponsor. But as the Scripture says, we've got to "die to self" to live. Paul cried, "I have been crucified with Christ; it is no longer I who live, but Christ who lives in me . . ." (Galatians 2:20 RSV). T. S. Eliot said, "In our end is our beginning."

"I give you the end of a Golden String, only wind it into a ball." Picking up the thread of this new way of life is not once and for all. Paul also said, "I die daily"; one is born into a "long, long trail a-winding." Alcoholics Anonymous, for instance, has detected twelve steps that are to be taken, and they are as valid for the spiritually arrogant as for the carnally addicted.

It is longer than the sawdust trail. We need not go around this world, but we must go through it. It has to do, as in those inspired twelve steps, not only with our

24

capitulating and turning our lives completely over to God, but with coughing up the specific roots of our special depravity to another person. It means leaving no stone unturned to make things right with each victim of our sins. Did you know that A.A.'s twelfth step calls for a spiritual awakening? That's more scriptural than church.

"It will take you in at Heaven's gate," the gate to the Garden we somehow lost. We make progress into a future, but paradoxically it is as though the past we lost is beyond the future. You cannot have been around the dying without recognizing their orientation to childhood. The aged do not suffer altogether from senility; it is homesickness. In the words of Wordsworth, "trailing clouds of glory do children come from God who is our home." Life is intended to make a full circuit. As the ball of Golden String grows in our hands there is the increasing awareness and overwhelming nostalgia for the beginning again.

Elisabeth Kübler-Ross has called attention to the huge significance of death as a front door and not simply an exit. While many of her examples who had had a brush with death looked back on their physical bodies as they left, as Blake and others had expressed it artistically long before, they were aware of a presence and an awesome enlargement of consciousness they longed for, leading them on. Sir Walter Scott died saying, "It's so good to be home."

Those who scorn heaven's gate never picked up the end of the Golden String. It is not entirely their fault. Their wish for death to be a wall, or their incapacity for faith, reveals the lack of someone else's love for them. Those who wander listlessly or resentfully in the labyrinth of despair are our fault, too, and have to do with our own imperfect hold on the Golden String. In the 1985 marathon in Madrid, of four thousand runners, two thirty-six-year-old friends led in the home stretch. Suddenly one was seized with cramps and could not go on until his partner put his arm around him. They crossed the finish line victors together.

That is the way to wind the Golden String. There are many races, roads, many different strings, since each of us must walk or run from his or her own unique origin. And while God does not despise any sincere string, some strings are better than others, and I believe we can be both tolerant and humble while still believing that there is a string of gold.

With all due respect to Confucianism, Confucius confessed to offering only a piece of string. His was a temporary path that he believed led nowhere except to the wall of death. He encountered no God at all. His recommendations were strictly confined to earth's brief summer. I studied under the American authority on Buddhism and hosted in my home the visit of the senior Buddhist in Southeast Asia in his saffron robe, during the heyday of my conviction that one religion was as good as another. But as I watched the sad face of the old monk, which was vowed never to look upon a woman, even withstanding my tumultuous three-year-old's insisting he look at her, it finally dawned on me that no one else even pretends to offer any truly competitive string. ". . . Lord, to whom shall we go? thou hast the words of eternal life" (John 6:68).

Buddhism essentially recommends suicide. It is all very serene and philosophical, but nonetheless urges death to all our desires, monitored by a noble eightfold path that leads to no gate, nor city, but to *Nirvana*, which in the Sanskrit literally means "extinguished." While paying tribute to Buddhists, who in many ways are more Christ-like than we are and, no thanks to us, have never known they had a choice, there is, in all honesty, only one "high way and a low, and each must choose the way his soul must go." I say this after also seeing what the practice of Islam has done in Iran.

John the Baptist, on the eve of his death, sent a message to Christ from prison: "Are You the One who is expected, or shall we look for another?" It is the question we all must ask. And after a lifetime, which has included living in the Far East, traveling all over the world, and burying myself deep in the stacks of libraries looking up the records of man's trek, I believe Jesus said it supremely the way it was, and forever is: "I am the way."

I am now convinced that no one who sincerely looks for God will reject Christ if He is offered in the right way. Most are already sick and tired of their broken strings of cotton or silk and would jump at the chance for a string that holds. Anyone truly seeking for God pants for Him like a thirsty antelope for water and will never refuse a drink of the real thing. Had I a firm enough grip on that true lifeline, and had I wound it tight enough, even my old Buddhist priest might have become as overjoyed as my distinguished Christian friend, a former Hindu.

Some so-called Christians can be obnoxious with their "I love Jesus" T-shirts, but God's Son was born about 1,987 years ago as even our calendars still record. And He was the only One who cared enough to die for us. Then, miracle of all miracles, without any other rival, He lived to lead us home.

The Good News is that this new Adam made it safely back into the Garden that we fled and promises us this *Paradise Regained*. And while the snake remains active—and life-threatening—his venomous head is mortally wounded. Whether Jerusalem's wall means some faraway celestial place, or "nearer than hands or feet," we pray "thy Kingdom come on earth as it is in heaven." No one knows, not the blessed angels, nor even the Son, the hour. We do not understand, and we cannot agree whether Eden was a geographical place in Mesopotamia, and our new Eden simply here on a different frequency, beyond Tolkien's "Middle Earth." Yet my heart has finally come to rest in the belief that: "Eye hath not seen, nor ear heard, neither have entered into the heart of man, the things which God hath prepared . . ." (1 Corinthians 2:9).

Keep winding the Golden String. There is no kite in the sky that tugs on the other end. It is in the hands of God.

2

My Father's
Servants
Live Better

*A*dam and Eve ended up somewhere *East of Eden* according to John Steinbeck's title, but we're so disillusioned now we do not know whether we're east or west of it, or whether it ever was. We are like shipwrecked solar mariners so lost in space we cannot remember the port from which we embarked. Like the younger son who fled to a far country, we, too, are immersed in an existence that has threatened our memory about any former idyllic state. Our amnesia has swallowed everything except a faint nostalgia for a better world.

As long as we think we're only a little east of where we should be and "perfectly capable of taking care of ourselves, thank you," we'll never know there's a way back. The sooner we stop deluding ourselves about our condition the better. As long as the old Indian insisted, "Indian not lost, wigwam lost," he could not pick up the trail. There is no hope until we know we are hopelessly lost. Only someone who admits he is lost will ever get excited by the end of a Golden String.

Surely we can tell by the wars we've been having that we've drifted into the wrong neighborhood. It is as though we've lost our minds as well as our way. Suddenly everybody seems to be playing with matches, and no one seems to care that we have sailed into a sea of gasoline. Tempers erupt volcanically with such pathological fury that George Bernard Shaw was forced to conclude, "If the other planets are inhabited, they must be using earth as their insane asylum."

As recently as a century ago we Americans massacred forty thousand of our own boys in one day at Antietam as though it were a sellout Rose Bowl. Most participants were Christians, and many had had the best education we could give them in the East. We not only burned down the Cotton Bowl, we almost broke up housekeeping altogether. America looked like a "far country" in those days, particularly behind Sherman's march from Atlanta to the sea. An awful lot of boys left home to go kill their kissing cousins; it was all in the family, and many never came back. We still manage to maintain the front of the "brave new world" but obviously we've been busy wandering in circles in the wilderness only a little better dressed than that mob of ex-convicts under Moses.

Now our whole world is cut in two by a curtain of iron instead of the Mason-Dixon line. And with two recent global war dress rehearsals already, along with the current epidemic of terrorism, there is no reason to think World War III cannot be completely "successful" for all sides.

If we default on the required military buildup, we can look forward to a savage bloodbath under ruthless tyranny such as is suffered not only by the helpless victims we abandoned in Vietnam but inevitably and irreversibly by everybody wherever the Communists have taken over. Fighting the Communists or yielding to them both seem intolerable. Somehow our planet appears lost and impatient to be swallowed by the black hole.

How ignorant and arrogant for New York to equate the "far country" with Lebanon or Johannesburg. Monstrous wrong must not get away with murder anywhere, but how ridiculous for some smug seminary or self-righteous denomination to jab a finger at a corporation or a storefront church.

Actually this runaway streak in us is endemic. You could pick any human being on earth and send him off to another planet as a good representative sample of what is wrong with earth. In fact, that is how the planet *Perelandra* is shadowed in the volume of space fiction by C. S. Lewis. This birth defect breeds true in each one of us. We're all recognizable children of a falling star. Earth is the "far country," and its tragic hero is the prodigal son, or his even more prodigal elder brother. God has three sons. The One is perfect. We're one of the other two; that story is earth's family album. It is our autobiography.

My great friend, Bob White, one of the founding fathers of Alcoholics Anonymous, told his dramatic life story to a

conference on the West Coast a few years ago. He introduced himself as a well-intentioned misfit from birth. His
problem was that he was powerless. He wanted to be
good, to do right. He just didn't have the power. When he
was ten his father gave him a jackass. Shortly after
receiving this prize there was a revival in the little Baptist
church across the road from where they lived in west
Texas. His father led the choir and his mother played the
piano.

Bob was bored during the revival and decided he could
slip out of the service unnoticed, go check on his new
burro, and be back in his seat before anyone knew the
difference. However, petting wasn't enough; he had to
ride it around the barn. Before he knew it that jackass was
out of control and on his way into the church despite
everything the frantic boy could do. Once inside, the beast
proceeded to do the only thing left that could be worse
than entry. While four Baptist deacons cleaned that up,
Bob said, his father unseated him faster than he ever
remembered before or since.

Bob White confessed that incident as the perfect exposure of his mortal life. He was as powerless over himself as
over that unruly jackass.

As a young man he discovered liquor to be a form of
power. It gave him enough of the illusion of power that he
managed to fool himself for a long time, although the
disastrous cost finally brought him to the breaking point.

During his last fling, Bob told his wife he was not going
to drink anymore. Following this announcement they
stopped at a bar. She ordered a coke, and he ordered a
crème de menthe. She said, "I thought you said you were
not going to drink anymore." "I'm not," he replied. "Only
crème de menthe from now on."

He drank half a gallon of crème de menthe a day—at times even a gallon. The whites of his eyes finally took on a green tint. So did the armpits of his shirts. When he wiped perspiration from his forehead, it made a green smudge on his handkerchief. One day his wife showed him his shorts from the laundry. They were turning green. No matter how much alcohol he took, or tried not to take, he was still powerless.

Finally he took the first steps in the twelve-steps program of Alcoholics Anonymous:

1. We admitted we were powerless over alcohol—that our lives had become unmanageable.
2. We came to believe that a power greater than ourselves could restore us to sanity.
3. We made a decision to turn our will and our lives over to God as we understood Him.

That was years ago, and I don't suppose we could count the number of desperate addicts that Bob White has led from death to the life from which he has never stepped back. Bob has reached a profound conclusion that applies to every human being. It is thoroughly New Testament although I've never heard anyone else say it. "Human beings are not able to choose between right and wrong. The only choice any of us have is God—or not."

"Thine is the Kingdom and the *power*," as Saint John said it: "He was in the world, and the world was made by him, and the world knew him not. He came unto his own, and his own received him not. But as many as received him, to them gave he power . . ." (John 1:10–12).

We must recognize that the sober elder brother who stayed at home and never missed church was as lost as the prodigal. It may take the "good" elder brother longer to realize he's lost cold sober at home, but he actually is as bad off as Cain, with enough jealousy to kill his brother or wish him dead or that he hadn't come back. What's the difference?

This is why the world is about to blow. There aren't any good guys, and the "good guys" don't know it. The elder brother is really the worse villain of the two. He represents the decent, law-abiding citizen. The elder brother stays out of trouble, but he never finds anything to apologize for, or be thankful for. The prodigal spends his way to hell; the elder brother saves his way there.

The villains in the New Testament, in almost all of Jesus' forty stories—including the people who arranged for Christ to be crucified—resembled the elder brother. He is hopelessly lost in his own neat room, with his religion arranged to suit his best interests. The elder brother doesn't know, or won't admit, he's lost. Why should he be looking for any Golden String? Everything will be just fine as soon as everyone else shapes up like him.

Bad as "the knife and revolver people" are, or the drunks and the lawbreakers, they really are more moral than the majority of "decent" folks. For instance, the crime wave of a sleepy little town in the Bible Belt is mild compared to the unmentionable intramural feuds that come to a head in church meetings there or sneak under the door of their "respectable" homes. The iniquity I speak of is of no interest to the newspaper or the court-room. The "good guys" get away with murder "in the bosom of the family by attrition," as Albert Camus uncovers it in *The Fall.*

Our hell on earth between nations doesn't come out of

the blue; it is accumulated from the expertise we acquire in church and home. The most horrid calamity of the day is not the riot in Brussels or the scandal at the Pentagon, not even the winos clustered around Central Park. It is, for instance, the newscaster's own hidden hell. He's shaking his head, along with us viewers, over the marketable disasters he's scraped up to feed our curiosity. However, God is interested in, and the devil is most active in, the newscaster's dislike or neglect of his own daughter, or his preference for her sister, or perhaps the true story of what he did to his ex-wife, or what he had to do to the former newscaster in order to land his job. The far country is fabricated from all these tolerated and unnewsworthy sins in our deepest hearts.

It is so much easier to bury or dismiss the basic wrong in each of our malfunctioning hearts and to play this game of getting upset over a selection of agreed-upon dramatic instances of wrong. But the national symptoms we feature in the media have all ballooned from these semi-secret seeds of our own discontent. No doubt that lost boy in Jesus' story, as well as his more cunning elder brother, also idled away his eligibility, shaking his head over an arbitrary selection of sinners we've all decided to discriminate against.

Camus goes on in *The Fall* to unmask the best of us as the worst, as the story of the Prodigal Son suggests. The martyrdom of the saints was a mild infraction compared to the daily output of "put-downs" of others that most of us exhale as commonly as carbon monoxide. With everyone nibbling on one another like piranha, we can all be finished off with winks and raised eyebrows, without any nuclear assistance at all. Our maliciousness can reign unchecked while we're distracted by the media. I see the elder brother as a type of person who hides a heart filled with hate behind his public charity and his prayers for the needy. He has ingeniously placed himself conveniently above help.

In Jesus' masterful account both boys are lost, signifying that all the world is lost, but it is the prodigal who grasps how desperate our situation is and points the way:

> Before very long, the younger son collected all his belongings and went off to a distant land, where he squandered his wealth in the wildest extravagance. And when he had run through all his money, a terrible famine arose in that country, and he began to feel the pinch. Then he went and hired himself out to one of the citizens of that country who sent him out into the fields to feed the pigs. He got to the point of longing to stuff himself with the husks the pigs were eating, and not a soul gave him anything. Then he came to his senses and cried aloud, "Why, dozens of my father's hired men have more food than they can eat and here am I dying of hunger! I will get up and go back to my father. . . ."
>
> Luke 15:13–18 PHILLIPS

There is a way out. Someone has thrown us a golden lifeline to God. Now we go back to the first man on earth who pioneered this journey homeward.

3

The First
Search
for the
Lost City

*I*f earthlings blame Adam and Eve for getting us lost, we have Abraham to thank for being the first castaway who "came to himself" in this far country. He not only began the comeback but blazed the way for all of us. After all those controversial epochs that went up in the smoke of despair, certainly dimming the memory of any paradise that could once have been, this incredible pioneer of our faith obeyed the longing in his heart for some nameless city and set out on the remarkable journey this book reports.

And if Adam is the first man in the Bible, Abraham is the first man in history now generally accepted by secular scholars too. He lived near Baghdad almost two thousand years before Christ. And while we have ancient records from Egypt and the Far East long predating Abraham, he is the first person history thoroughly introduces. Certainly he's the first to respond memorably to our abduction, or whatever you choose to call our mortal predicament.

No doubt Abraham had tried many gods in his native city of Ur, hoping to hitch a ride back. But he found that the gods were not only as lost as he was, they were also oblivious to it. They specialized exclusively in local color, such as rain or fertility.

While they all had strings attached, they were strings that bound men like leashes. The gods and their priests lived off folks and multiplied like fleas. Abraham saw through them. None of them were capable of getting anyone out of town, for their power waned, like that of radio transmitters, as you left the vicinity of their local shrines.

It became obvious to this star-mad man that all the sackfuls of gods stacked on the merchants' shelves or painstakingly arranged on family hearths were completely ludicrous before this emergency of life and death staring us in the face. The utter futility of these expensive religions limping and moaning helplessly around him broke Abraham open to suggestion from a higher power. The situation screamed for a comprehensive God who cared. It demanded the very God from whom they had all gotten lost. Who else could make any sense out of the jagged pieces of life or ever fit them back together as originally intended?

We are all familiar with the fabulous accomplishments of migrating birds, which annually bring some of them north from the tropics many hundreds of miles, often to be sighted year after year on the same limb on the same day in April. Therefore, we ought not to write off Abraham as eccentric for possibly possessing some superior homing instinct.

After all our sophisticated digging, the recent knowledge of our origins is still quite infantile, with more than one link still missing in the sequence of prehistoric events. Then why are we so naive for taking seriously someone who sensed we were displaced persons? Abraham began tracking his way back to our entrance spiritually, and his pilgrimage has stood up well for a long time under heavy fire.

We are not unappreciative of the theory of evolution. It has a powerful hold on all modern minds. But it is only a theory. And while it appeals to us for many of the wrong reasons, including the way it salves our egos in putting our forebears beneath us, I now find myself fascinated by the possibility that those who assembled the Bible, and began it with Eden, also had good reasons.

Abraham, who suffered in ignorance of some of our contemporary boasts, possessed more modesty about his hometown, believing others before him might have done better. Rather than writing off his forebears as Flintstones and Neanderthals, he found himself instead revering his origin, as though he had fallen from a previous height. Abraham's perspective is a rare and refreshing one. We might do well to let it season ours.

In the twelfth chapter of Genesis, the God this God-sick man was looking for reached him. It was his kind of God—not wordy and wanting silver, but brief, and all He wanted was Abraham. These were God's first words to him as recorded in Genesis 12:1–3 (NKJV):

39

Get out of your country . . . and from your father's house,
to a land that I will show you. I will make you a great
nation . . . and in you all the families of the earth shall be
blessed.

This was no memorial inscription to a mantelpiece God.
The voice embarked Abraham on the trip for which he'd
been born.

Abraham was not a prodigal in the sense of a wastrel
but rather the first of us to waken from some kind of jet lag
and to scout "back to the future" as a recent film was
entitled. Abraham was no programmed religious robot.
He was only human, but an undeniable hope had somehow taken root in him. So, armed with unbelievable
courage and trust, ". . . he went out, not knowing where
he was to go" (Hebrews 11:8 RSV).

Perhaps Abraham stood in his doorway one morning,
his feet webbed with the strings that tied up his city. They
led nowhere except into Gordian knots that would have
yielded no meaning even had Alexander cut them with his
sword. This time, standing in the quiet dawn as though in
a dream, he perceived something more clearly than ever
before; to use Blake's metaphor, the end of a strange string
was sparkling at his feet. It stretched down the walk in
front of him and into the distance beyond. Things had
been building in Abraham for years. The reflection of the
sunlike string was almost blinding as the dawn struck it
that morning.

Can we imagine an event more significant for earth than
this one lone man refusing to remain in the ruts in which
his neighbors were caught and declaring that we were

wayfarers, that earth really is only a one-night stand? We have to move. And right in front of Abraham Someone had somehow thrown the charted course he was looking for: the Word of God.

After what must have seemed an eternity (how many such mornings did it take?), Abraham turned back into the house and gave instructions to his head servant, still rubbing sleep from his eyes, "Make immediate preparations for departure. We're leaving for good in the morning." Then Abraham went back into the house to pack and to ponder what a weird and wonderful thing he was doing. Would it make such a difference to the world in the long run? He had nothing better to do.

This new God who spoke to Abraham was Elohim, the first God whose power was not lost on one locality. He was a traveler's God, a God on the run, not a sedentary God. El was the kind of God the lost man needs, a God capable of using string to guide one to a water hole and eventually all the way to the place where we will never thirst again. The gods usually lived in one-room shacks, supposedly able to defend about as much acreage as a blue jay, but this God was the One who would later be referred to as having a mansion of many rooms, the God of the heavens and the earth.

Abraham "looked for a city which hath foundations, whose builder and maker is God" (Hebrews 11:10). Abraham had had enough of cities without foundations. In fact, the chapter in Genesis previous to those about Abraham reported the destruction of the tower of Babel that men had proudly jerry-built on their own. Apparently its crash was the last straw for Abraham. He wouldn't stand for any more crash programs. It would be all or nothing, in a city that couldn't fall.

So Abraham went over the heads of all the usual developers. The best were not good enough to build his home. His would be put up to stay—whatever it took. What a breakthrough. For the first time someone grasped: "Except the Lord build the house, they labour in vain that build it . . ." (Psalms 127:1). The contract to do it was extreme. We still call it the Old Covenant, or Old Testament. And that deal was made forever, for all of us. It was made between Abraham and the One we shall call, until the day we die, not the God of Adam, nor the God of Noah, but the God of Abraham.

Basically this unbreakable bond meant that Abraham would obey the God of his house, and God would build the house of Abraham into quite a place, until it spilled over with children as the sky spills over with stars. Unusually grand specifications even for a builder, but this was the "Builder and Maker." Eventually every male child would be circumcised as a reminder of how deep this contract with God had cut into us.

However, there was one very strange thing about Abraham's homeowner's policy. Abraham was left holding something like a piece of string in his hands. It never led him to any physical house. Abraham took it all on faith according to the Book of Hebrews:

By faith he sojourned in the land of promise, as in a foreign land, living in tents with Isaac and Jacob, heirs with him of the same promise. For he looked forward to the city which has foundations, whose builder and maker is God.

Hebrews 11:9, 10 RSV

After all these house plans, Abraham would remain a camper on the earth. He behaved like a refugee. He bought no property as long as he lived—except a cave for burial. Abraham had astronomic aspirations. Earth is not the objective. Man doesn't belong here. Abraham had seen enough of that kind of thinking back in Ur. And he saw Lot's wife—and very nearly Lot himself—turn to sodium by staying too long and sitting too tight in Sodom. Abraham's string did not end in those cities. It led to the City of God.

So Abraham never lived in a house again after he left Ur. If you had asked him for his address, that old exile would have replied in the words of Hebrews: "For here have we no continuing city, but we seek one to come" (Hebrews 13:14).

This is why Abraham had been able to give Lot first choice of the land. Lot took the fertile plains and Abraham the leftover hill country partly because a big hunk of earth did not matter that much to Abraham. Abraham would simply not be taken in by this "first room" in his father's house—in fact, this was the room, ". . . from thy father's house . . ." (Genesis 12:1), that was not for staying.

Scholars often insist that the Old Testament, as the Orthodox Jews interpret it and certainly the Sadducees if not the Pharisees, does not enjoy belief in life after death. They believe that the only reward offered is long life here, and that after that the best of us must go down to Sheol. That is untrue. While much of it may be implicit, eternal paradise is implied in the story of the Garden of Eden itself. It is in Job, whether added later or not. Even Enoch, before Abraham appeared, was whisked away to a preferable estate without the bother of death.

But the life to come is ever so powerful a motif in the story of Abraham. This "pie on the ground" never for a minute satisfied him. His mobile caravan in the midst of land all given to him is unmistakable witness to a land afar.

Of course the stupendous event in all of Abraham's life was the late arrival of the son God had promised and seemed to have forgotten. Abraham possessed one virtue almost unknown to us addicts of drive-in fast foods: *patience*. It is another mark of a believer in "other rooms."

Then there was laughter. People who don't know any better, attribute to God solemnity, and to a patriarch ponderousness. Actually God played His part of the Old Testament almost as a practical joke. Not until after Sarah was ninety and Abraham pushing a century did God let Sarah become pregnant.

And Abraham's reaction to that announcement was no long-faced "Let us pray." Abraham laughed his head off. Genesis 17:17 reads: "Then Abraham fell upon his face, and laughed. . . ." How could anybody that old laugh that hard about anything? And the boy born to those aged parents was named Isaac, which in Hebrew meant *laughter*. That signifies that Abraham was on to the string, for the gods back in Ur never laughed like that.

The baby boy was no sooner a lad than the Lord wanted him back—by Abraham's own hand. Authorities sigh that it had to do with the contemporary practice of sacrifice of the firstborn which was common among the Canaanites. Perhaps it did, but it is also the most powerful example of faith ever recorded. Far more people than Kierkegaard have been transfixed before it as with nothing else in the Old Testament. No one who believes that God is God will fail to learn what faith is from Abraham's willingness to sacrifice the beloved son he'd waited for all his life. By this act he fathered the chosen people. The first commandment would be, "Thou shalt have no other gods before me!" Abraham showed what it took to keep that command ahead of time so that God Himself would have no reason left to deny us the City.

Wherever you and I are at this point in our own journey, we can now be sure that there is a point to our journey, because of this old man's devotion to our destiny. Abraham was no saint. He struggled and fought like us. He once abandoned his wife Sarah to Pharaoh, saying she was his sister to save his own skin. He never made it to heaven and back so we could be certain. However, his life still stands as an incredible lesson in trust. He trusted, withholding nothing. That is the way he turned everyone's life into a journey.

Abraham turned death into a journey. He interpreted earth as a path that leads somewhere. Earth is a ball of bright string; he unraveled it so we could find our way to God.

As William Cullen Bryant looked at the migrating wildfowl in the autumn sky he versed this belief that life is a flight, a path to somewhere.

> He who from zone to zone
> Guides through the boundless sky thy certain
> flight,
> In the long way that I must tread alone,
>   Will lead my steps aright.

4

The Practice
Run to
the Promised
Land

$\mathcal{A}$braham was only the beginning, and like all good stories the Old Old Story has had its ups and downs. About five hundred years after Abraham, that new string broke in Egypt, or so it seemed. The house of Abraham caught so much hell down there that his descendants began to think any ultimate rendezvous with God was an empty dream.

Abraham's son, Isaac, and Isaac's son, Jacob, took their turns successfully, but Jacob's son, Joseph, aroused so much envy in his brothers that they sold him up the Nile into slavery. However, that proved to be a blessing in disguise. For that suffering as a slave boy, and later as a convict, made Jacob's spoiled brat into such a sage that Pharaoh made him co-king. Then, as though it had all been arranged, when famine struck old Jacob back in the now unpromising land, there was Joseph, already beside the Pharaoh with his barns full, ready to forgive and feed his bloody brothers as fast as they could get there. Some string.

Next, we took the second hard fall; this time from Abraham's makeshift Eden, the Promised Land, which seemed for a long time to extend as far as Egypt. But Egypt proved to be an exorbitant price to pay for Joseph's pantry, unless one believes we really are getting somewhere.

Long after Joseph and the good king died, a royal monster crawled onto the Egyptian throne and began wiping his feet with Israelites. He not only enslaved them but swatted them like flies when they failed to come up with impossible quotas of straw-deficient bricks. It was torment calculated to turn them away from God. Finally he ordered a massacre of all Hebrew boy babies. After that it became dangerous to mention the name of Abraham. The ball of string had apparently been buried with Joseph long before.

One Hebrew mother had enough hope left to abandon her baby to the bulrushes. She sent him off in a tiny boat tarred with pitch to where the princess took her daily bath. Such resourcefulness fooled the Egyptian police then as it fools skeptics now. That mother thought of everything, even to having the infant's sister, Miriam, standing by to suggest just the right wet nurse. So the princess reared him as her own and named him Moses, which meant she pulled him out of the river.

This account of the birth of Moses is not sabotaged simply because it is also associated with the origin of another ancient figure. In fact, when one attempts to account for the impact Moses has had upon our pilgrimage this birth story is altogether too modest. Whether or not another mother rehearsed or repeated it hardly rids us of the perfect timing and placement of Moses' arrival. But Moses' parentage pales into insignificance beneath the lengthening shadow this man has cast over all who are making this trek to Jerusalem's wall.

Somehow this Hebrew appeared whose spirit had not been beaten out of him in the brickyards, who seemed bred to beard a Ramses in his den. As soon as Moses discovered he was a legitimate son of the scum that Pharaoh was sweeping underfoot, he murdered an Egyptian officer for brutality against one of them. This landed Moses on the king's wanted list, so he took off for the land of Midian, a young king with no kingdom.

Moses found himself in an oasis where several girls were unable to water their flocks because rough trail drivers kept bullying them out of their turn. Moses befriended the girls so successfully that their father gave him one of them to keep and took him into the family business. The exiled prince could have remained in that hideout forever.

However, the helpless victims Moses had abandoned back in Egypt began groaning to God, for their burden had become too great to bear. Soon Moses was wanted by God as well as by Pharaoh. So God set up an ambush to get him.

Moses was hard to get, but God never has seemed interested in anyone who is easy to catch. The saga of the unique string is packed with unexpected, even difficult company. God goes to a great deal of trouble to get people, partly because God wants to make clear He is doing it and also because He wants to secure a commitment not already fatigued by too many trifling religious exercises.

So God ordered an angel to set up an interview. That is why Moses stumbled onto a bush that was blazing away but not being burned up. That kindled Moses' return to Egypt for the desperate folks he'd left behind.

Moses was very reluctant to be in the Bible. He talked back: "Who are you?" The bush replied, "The God of Abraham." Moses wanted more credentials, and God came on with enough dossier for the One who didn't have to answer to anyone: "I am that I am." Moses realized he would still seem a fool in front of a Pharaoh who was under the impression that he too was God, to say nothing of trying to convince the bitter pessimists he represented. "I'll be with you." "But I stutter." "Your brother, Aaron, can do the talking."

That is how the man next to God himself was inserted into what we still call to this day the Book of Moses. God will have innumerable helpers before the golden ball is wound, but this credentialed athlete who spoke Egyptian with the royal accent, who was as at ease in a palace as in a tent, and who possessed both the nerve and the compassion to break the neck of tyranny, was the one on whom rested God's first major rescue attempt.

Whether Pharaoh was Ramses II, who we know reigned about that time for sixty-seven years, lived a century, and fathered 150 children, or another, we know that a Pharaoh was a handful. Napoleon's servants measured Ramses' ear where his statue still lies in the sand. It was three and a half feet long. Influencing any of these lords of the Nile was like pushing against a cliff.

When Moses suggested that Pharaoh dismiss the Hebrews, Pharaoh took it as a joke. Moses' colorful little visits amused him. Pharaoh's own magicians even mimicked Moses' miracles with a trick or two. It was not going to be easy to shake the colossal confidence of one of these lordly beings who tossed eternal pyramids along the Nile as they went by.

Moses did ten things to get some respect. Whatever problems the plagues present, the Exodus becomes even more of a mystery without them. They made enough of an impression on suspicious Jews to win ten flicks of wine with the finger every year at Passover forever. I joined Jewish friends last spring to see it done for about the 3200th time. I take that to be an authoritative footnote.

First, Moses turned the sacred Nile red as blood. No luck. Next he infested Egypt with frogs until they infiltrated the king's bed at night. But apparently the king enjoyed Bloody Mary's and frog legs. He was not someone who could be pestered easily. Then Moses struck out with clouds of gnats, quickly following with thousands of acres of insects, and as if the poor cattle hadn't had enough, he covered them with an exclusive pestilence. All these theatrics of nature seemed to entertain Pharaoh, for apparently his own court dramatists seemed incapable of incorporating biology so completely in their productions.

Then Moses began raising boils, even on the necks of the priests, which was rather reckless for those fellows were accustomed to preferential treatment and without their offices one could be denied embalming. But by this time Moses was rapidly getting to the bottom of the most impressive arsenal of weapons with which anyone had ever been armed. Nine out of ten seemed futile. Moses gave them hail, blew drifts of locusts across their fields, and just before the tenth disaster, he put the sun out. But all that had no more life-changing effect than when Cecil B. DeMille and Charlton Heston did it on the screen.

Moses was simply opening Pharaoh's eyes and rehearsing his people for the main event. The tenth plague was the heartbreaker. Getting his timing right, Moses announced that at midnight the firstborn son of every family in Egypt would die. The only exceptions to this unprecedented calamity being Hebrew families who had dined that night on roasted lamb and smeared the blood over the front door (Exodus 12:23, 29). The death angel would pass over those houses marked by the blood of the lamb.

That midnight, precisely as Moses had predicted, such a moan rose from the throats of the Egyptians as has never been heard before or since, including the palace itself where the crown prince had fallen; Moses at last got through to Pharaoh. At that final blow Pharaoh banished the Hebrews from Egypt, and they left under Moses in such a rush that the bread did not have time to rise. They took the unleavened bread with them, and it would always remain a reminder.

This tenth plague was so crucial to the recovery of the Golden String, and so influential an event for all the people who have ever lived on the face of the earth, that God made it a commandment to repeat the Passover in a ceremony every year. That this has been done for over three thousand years is a stupendous miracle in itself, as well as overwhelming testimony to its having taken place.

Taking on Pharaoh was only practice for Moses to take on the Red Sea which blocked their escape better than bricks. While the Hebrews pondered this barrier the dust rose at their backs from Pharaoh's pursuing chariot wheels. There they were, pinched between the Nemesis of the Nile and the deep Red Sea, which is as sharp a picture of our mortal predicament today as one could find.

So it was here in history, while death had this mob of ex-convicts completely surrounded, with no possible way out, that God moved in for all to see forever after. Even as the people were ready to stone Moses for saving them for this, Moses still had enough faith left to say, "Stand still and see the salvation of the Lord."

It was the most inappropriate time for thanksgiving imaginable when the string shone so gloriously. Moses split the sea in two with the rod in his hand, and the people walked across the corridor provided without getting their feet wet. Then, when Ramses and his soldiers tried it, Moses shut the waters with no more effort than closing a door. And that was the end of the chase.

Such a crossing of that usually uncooperative body of water very nearly upstaged the Passover associated with it. There is no way of getting rid of these two momentous events, for I have tried. If one were somehow able to eradicate them from history it would make Moses' escape all the more remarkable, and would require an even more fantastic system of transportation to ferry them out of Egypt.

The memories that kept them going ever after came from something. Was it not the inspiration of these two keepsakes which no amount of ridicule or forgetfulness have managed to erase? They suggest that He'll make a gate through the last wall of the final city we seek.

Pharaoh and the Red Sea were modest challenges to Moses compared to the riot of relatives he was supposed to lead. How could any modern scholar regard himself as less naive than this society of suspicious kinfolk that coagulated about Moses. The Bible's chief kibitzers are within its pages. How could anyone still believe that people are essentially good after their indecent exposure in Exodus, where the Hebrews luxuriated in the most dazzling spiritual splendors of all time? It would be difficult for earth to stoop any lower than did those obnoxious ingrates who dogged Moses' heels in the very shadow of Sinai.

This wilderness they determined to linger in was conspicuously unprovisioned, even without drinking water, stocked with poisonous snakes, and had a climate more conducive to despair than the perpetual polar night. But it was this exasperating sand trap that practically produced the Pentateuch. This back-door exit from Egypt that Moses found became a perfect foil for Moses' memory verses. The Hebrews were assigned forty years of this hard lesson, because of their lack of faith to enter the Promised Land.

The pillars of fire that led them by night were nothing compared with waking up every day to bread raining down on their heads. A drink of water out there took one's breath away, for all you knew it came out of rock. Those forty years the Israelites suffered in that stronghold of fear compiled an album over which such glory hovers that we still find in its pages Him who leads us now. That they made it at all is stupefying; that they made that long haul into Scripture cannot long be pondered safely by an unbeliever. In such an odyssey of survival, miracles such as manna are minimum concessions. I have come at last to understand that I would be the most gullible man on earth to believe that the Israelites got through that wilderness unassisted.

The most memorable feature of this Exodus was Moses' ascent to Sinai to pick up the ten ground rules that would civilize the world. Several of those that have escaped us come back to me now as I go over them again, particularly the fierce objections against false witness and covetousness. There's nothing worse now, nothing more characteristic of us, than these two sins; nothing threatens the peace of the world more than disregard of these two commands.

Our profanity, our idolatry of work, our incapacity to sit still are soundly condemned in these ten insights that glisten with newness still and, like buoys, still mark our way safely over those same eternal reefs.

Scholars sometimes depreciate Moses' contribution as lawgiver because others, such as Hammurabi, duplicated some of his laws. Egypt's saintly king, Ikhnaton, also perceived that God was One. Many wise men may have influenced Moses under God. But God made Moses man enough to admit that these laws were not manmade, but spoken directly to his heart by the same One who had spoken to him that day when the flaming bush turned him heavenward.

Whatever similar insights twinkled in cultural isolation up dead-end streets, this momentous occasion eclipsed them. This people were chosen, and their pilgrimage was selected as the highway by which these laws would travel west to us. It is a moment that takes history's breath away when Moses heard God say, in whatever way, "Thou shalt have no other gods before me. Thou shalt not make unto thee any graven image . . ." (Exodus 20:3, 4).

Moses' supreme discovery has been buried among all the legislative footnotes his scribes felt necessary to include. And this discovery takes Moses far beyond a lawgiver and into a shadow of the Saviour yet to come. When Moses returned from his forty-day trip up Sinai with his arms full of the heavy correspondence from God, he found everybody dancing about a golden calf. He broke the tablets and had people killed in his anger, revealing some of the savagery that makes the Old Testament so difficult for us.

But Moses' rage fades before one of the most magnificent scenes in all of recorded history. In his agony over what had happened, Moses said the prayer that more than anything else makes me think he was on to the string that would turn to gold: "O God, this people have sinned a great sin . . . yet now, if thou wilt forgive their sin—; and if not, then blot me . . . out of thy book which thou hast written" (Exodus 32:31, 32).

No wonder it is said that when Moses returned from Sinai with the tablets for the second time "written with the finger of God," his face shone with such brightness that the people were afraid to go near him.

Like Abraham, Moses, too, never had a permanent home on earth. He was literally found in the river, a refugee child reared by a foster mother in the palace. He went into self-imposed exile after his murder of the overseer and spent the rest of his life in the Exodus. And in the end, while he was permitted to watch everyone cross over into the Promised Land to which he had safely led them, he was not allowed to enter because of the time he failed to give the glory to God for the water coming out of the rock.

Perhaps Moses also did this to himself, for this quality of being able to give the glory to God was what distinguished Moses from all the other ancient kings. Moses was the only one of them who, instead of grabbing the throne for himself, acknowledged God as King. So if Moses felt he didn't deserve to go into the land he'd tried for a lifetime to give his people, God decided to take him to that far more blessed land toward which Moses led the world more than he knew. In fact, "there arose not a prophet since in Israel like unto Moses, whom the Lord knew face to face" (Deuteronomy 34:10).

So now, as we look both to the right and to the left to find our way, look back and, in the words of T. S. Eliot, "let your memory lead you." For this spectacular march of Abraham and Moses was no wild-goose chase, but a preview of the doom of our destroyer and a portent that death too is a door.

5

Follow Me

Moses died, "Joshua fit the battle of Jericho, and the walls came a tumblin' down" in that southernmost city. Soon the rest of the Promised Land was recovered. Eventually David occupied the place where Abraham had offered up Isaac, incorporating it into the Holy City of Jerusalem. Solomon built a sumptuous throne there for God, completing that site as the silhouette of the city we are seeking.

All the unmentionable things that men have done have not effaced that city as the symbol of our ultimate destination. Job took life on the chin but it did not break his belief in this. At one dark time Elijah alone was left against Queen Jezebel and her battalion of belligerent priests of Baal. Elijah, too, would have gone down had it not been for "a still small voice" that took its place in the threads of the brightening string.

At one point nothing but a beautiful queen was between us and oblivion. It was enough. Queen Esther asked every Israelite still standing to fast and pray for her for three days. Then she took her life in her hands to save them all, saying, "If I perish, I perish." It worked. Sampson used his great strength, Ruth her loyalty, and Hosea found out how far God would go for us by how many times he found himself forgiving his faithless wife. And it was Isaiah who reached for the star long before it shone so bright for three wise kings.

The One Isaiah saw coming was a son of Abraham and a son of David. He not only "for us men and our salvation came down from heaven," He was furnished by these same people; out of the furnace of their affliction He was born. Even when He taught He seldom made it up out of His own head but quoted heavily from all that His fathers had learned, just as on the third day after His death:

And beginning at Moses and all the prophets, he expounded unto them in all the scriptures the things concerning himself. . . . These are the words which I spake unto you, while I was yet with you, that all things must be fulfilled, which were written in the law of Moses, and in the prophets, and in the psalms, concerning me. Then

opened he their understanding, that they might understand the scriptures.

Luke 24:27, 44, 45

As would be expected of the One who commanded us,
"Follow me," He too was not made at home here. As He
Himself said, "The foxes have holes, and the birds of the
air have nests; but the Son of man hath not where to lay
his head" (Matthew 8:20). Saint John introduced Jesus as
homeless. "He was in the world, and the world was made
by him, and the world knew him not. He came unto his
own, and his own received him not" (John 1:10, 11).

When will we, too, grasp that this old earth is only our
path. There was, as Luke (2:7) said at His birth, ". . . no
room for them. . . ." Even His borrowed grave was to be
only a temporary resting place. Abraham, Moses, and
Jesus never gravitated to a permanent address on earth.
Home is at the end of the string He turned to gold for us.

Lest we remain rooted under the tree, caught in a circle
of Christmases, we must stare at His life from beginning to
end until we leave His cradle and move on to the Cross.
We call it the Way. The Old Old Story is not simply the
nativity scene; it is the street scene, and the mob scene
until we come to the place where we have seen enough to
see Him now. He is not only beside us but in "one of the
least of these." "The Word was made Flesh" and blood,
for us to follow "in His steps."

Doubt creeps in. And the doubt in His divinity is so
loud, the root of that heresy is doubt in His being one of
us down here. The Gnostics were the first, but today's
Thomas, for all his problems with the virgin birth, depre-

ciates any birth at all. Jesus has become ethereal, more like an angel than a man. And one cannot believe in God's Son if he doesn't believe in Him as our brother. Christmas comes before Easter can.

Ever since Voltaire was shocked in the eighteenth century when he overheard men discussing whether Jesus might be only make-believe, an army of experts has been digging back into the records and deep into the ruins to rediscover Him. Critics have called the evangelists themselves back to the witness stand and have subjected their testimony to the most merciless cross-examination that any words have ever received.

This investigation has not stopped with "inside information." The life and works of complete strangers were combed for every shred of evidence. A star witness was discovered in Josephus, the Jewish historian who about A.D. 90 volunteered that there was a man named Jesus, "if it be lawful to call Him a man, for He was a doer of wonderful works."[1] And after piecing together clues left in the correspondence of several leading Romans,[2] it became increasingly evident that Jesus not only lived but that the Gospel was far more accurate than our wildest dreams.

The wife of C. S. Lewis, Joy Davidman, was converted from Communism to Christianity, declaring that the inside evidence of the Gospels convinced her. She felt that no writers attempting to fake our faith would ever have come up with such things as twelve baskets left over after feeding the five thousand. Cutting off the soldier's ear would never have occurred to anyone unless Peter had done it. And if the resurrection of Jairus' daughter had been trumped up by a typical church promotion agent, there would have been a two-hour praise service. Instead, Jesus simply said, "Give her something to eat."

Dead Sea Scrolls and radioactive carbon tests certify the Bible's integrity in modern terms. The most fanatical skeptic has been forced at last to concede at least to Albert Schweitzer's conclusion in his *Quest of the Historical Jesus:* "The Gospel of Mark is in essentials genuine history." But what about those who knew Jesus best and were authorized to speak for Him?

Paul and Mark are silent about the night when Christ was born. But Matthew and Luke announce that it was five miles south of Jerusalem in the little town of Bethlehem. There were shepherds and kings, and there was Mary betrothed to the King of glory. These two writers do not act as if they were doctoring records, but as if they were trembling before a brighter light that had fallen upon them out of heaven from God. They painted with words something that could scarcely be put into words. Vandals have brutally attacked their "Virgin Story" as gross fabrication, but to the friends of Jesus it seemed "the masterpiece of understatement."

The babe was the firstborn of a large family of a backwoods Judean carpenter. Jesus was descended from Rahab, the prostitute, and Ruth, the Gentile (Matthew 1:5). They named the boy Joshua, "the help of God," which the Greeks and Romans rounded off to "Jesus."[3]

After Herod died, the holy family moved back from Egypt where they had fled to their hometown, Nazareth. It had an excellent water supply that is still known as "The Virgin's Well." The hill at the edge of town offered a magnificent view of snowcapped Mount Hermon to the east, and of Mount Carmel, warm with the memories of

Elijah, to the west. The Lad must have walked out there and looked up many times, for His parables feature fields of wild flowers and farmers going out to sow.

Mary gave Him several sisters and four brothers: James, Joses, Judas, and Simon. Each Sabbath He went to the synagogue (Luke 4:16) and heard the law read, first in Hebrew then translated into His native Aramaic.[4] He must have paid close attention and done His homework, for He was so steeped in what "they said unto you of old time" as to stagger the professors when He was twelve, and to stump the experts in the end.

After that time when Jesus was truant in the temple, Joseph is never mentioned in the New Testament again. So it is assumed that he died soon after, leaving the responsibilities as head of the house to fall early on the shoulders of the eldest Son. However short His father's life, Jesus affectionately chose the word *Father* as His favorite name for God. And if one worships the Son, it is difficult not to deify His mother; for His homelife provided the highest education ever offered. It was under that humble roof that He grew in such stature as to make Nathanael's question "Can there any good thing come out of Nazareth?" (John 1:46) the most famous last words.

Jesus left home to join John the Baptist. In the fifteenth year of the reign of Tiberius, A.D. 28, this rough outdoorsman, John, was northeast of the Dead Sea wearing camel's hide, eating dried locusts, and preaching ". . . the wrath to come" (Matthew 3:7). John was Jesus' second cousin, probably His closest boyhood friend. Jesus thought more of John than of any other man living or dead (Matthew 11:11). He asked John to baptize Him. Something happened to the two young men during the ceremony—

something that the whole world would never forget. Jesus left John standing there and fled to the wilderness to try to find Himself in the blinding light. But out there the light went out, and He was tempted in every way we are (Hebrews 4:15).

After John's imprisonment Jesus stepped in to fill his pulpit. The new preacher was different. John had been a rigid Essene who lived alone in a Jordan thicket. "The Son of man came eating and drinking . . ." (Matthew 11:19). To John, God's coming was a threat; to Jesus it was a promise: "The hour is at hand. Change your hearts and believe the Good News" (*see* Mark 1:15). He found Simon and Andrew fishing in Galilee. They were old friends, for they had all been friends of John. Jesus had a favor to ask and confer: "Follow me, and I will make you fishers of men." "Immediately they left their nets."

It was a moment to remember, for the Big Fisherman would be Jesus' second in command and would take over when He finished. They followed Jesus up the beach where they interrupted James and John mending their nets. At a word from Him they left their father and followed (Mark 1:19, 20). These four were all He called at first, and they were to be His closest friends until His dying day.

Apparently Jesus made His home with them for a while in Capernaum. They noticed that He awakened early and went off by Himself. He went with them to the synagogue on the Sabbath and was asked to speak. A maniac tried to break up the service, but something in the Guest Speaker's manner silenced the madman and stirred up everyone else. When they came home from church, they found Peter's mother-in-law in bed with a fever. At Jesus' touch the fever fled. News of that healing spread at the speed of light, and by sundown, when Jews were safe from Sabbath regulations, Peter's doorway was jammed with the damned (Luke 4:31–40).

That was only "opening night" for the explosive power pent up in Him. The hurt had such faith in Him that one bleeding woman asked only to touch the hem of His gown. One government official forgot his composure and shinnied up a sycamore to get a glimpse of His face. A highly respected Roman centurion stood before Him and said, "Lord, I am not worthy to have you come under my roof; but only say the word and my servant will be healed."

He drew such fantastic crowds that one patient had to be lowered through an opening in the ceiling to get His attention. Once the adoring multitude crowded Him into the sea, and He had to escape by boat. There was something about Him that made it very hard for men not to believe it was He who made the lame to walk and the blind to see. They gave Him no rest and He gave them no reason to believe He was not the One who was expected.

He cut His disciples down to twelve and taught them with parables and a prayer. And one day He questioned: "Who do you say that I am?" Peter blurted it out: "You are the Christ. . . ." Jesus confessed to it and broke the news that He would have to suffer for it. Peter could not take it, for he fantasized his Messiah mounted safely in military splendor. The roughness with which Jesus put Peter in his place perhaps betrays how difficult a decision it was for Him to make. Finally the three saw Him transfigured as "the suffering servant." What John had said made sense to them then: "Behold, the Lamb of God, who takes away the sin of the world!" (John 1:29 RSV.)

To Matthew, Christ is the crown and not the thorn of Jewish law. Much as Moses took his tablets down from Sinai, so the second Lawgiver delivered His ten beatitudes in a Sermon on the Mount. But Christ's edition of the Word punctured the ego and pricked the ire of Pharisees, and not even Matthew can hide their hatred. Christ's popularity alone was maddening enough, but He lost no opportunity to preach against their perpetual handwashing, their handwringing public prayers, their beautiful fronts, their ugly spirits.

Jesus became an outlaw to these legalists when He broke the Sabbath day to help someone and when He broke the caste system to sit down to eat with just anyone. They loathed Him for His love of life and little children, His longing for the lost, His limitless definition of neighbor, and His unheard of respect for women. They ground their teeth at such infuriating goodness and interrupted their minutia long enough to plot His destruction. The Sadducees caught Him and sent Him up to Pilate early one morning, officially on the charge of blasphemy, but actually because of that time He had whipped them from the temple.

Jesus had no intention of dying out there in the desert. He would win or lose in Jerusalem. He entered in triumph, not like a lamb but a lion. He made reservations for a colt to fulfill a prophecy and for a table to set a memory. The gospels give a day-by-day account of that last week. The climax crashed upon them from behind, for there at the condemned Man's last meal sat Judas with the rest. After supper they all sang together the customary Passover song from the Psalms. The last verse goes like this:

O give thanks unto the Lord for He is good: His mercy endureth forever.

He couldn't sleep and suggested a garden. When He arrived, He immediately excused Himself with the three and went farther in. They began to see something was going wrong. There He told them: "My heart is almost breaking! You must stay here and keep watch." They stayed and went to sleep. He went out of sight, but within hearing, and threw Himself to the ground and sobbed: "Father! Anything is possible for you! Take this cup away from me! Yet not what I please but what you do." The words were scarcely out of His mouth before the traitor crept up with the "cup" and gave Him away to the police with a kiss.

In a few more minutes all His friends gave Him up and fled. Peter got close enough to hear the rest—not close enough to keep the cock from crowing. He was man enough to admit it all to Mark; to weep bitterly how no man was with the Master at the last. Peter heard the unmerciful flogging administered in order to make the Cross more merciful. Then the thorns, spit, and trail of blood led to a spot not far from the north city wall. The last words that Peter heard from those cracked lips that day buried his heart beneath a stone that only God could roll away. The path Abraham had blazed was now paved in blood and glory. The string had become a street of gold.

Rome and Israel gnashed their teeth together upon the life of Christ. There was nothing more of Him to pick except His bones which they left hanging there. A poor man named Joseph had cradled Him in His first resting place. Now a rich man named Joseph lovingly carried Him to His last. Pilate sealed the tomb with a boulder and posted a soldier to guard the remains.

After three days, the three Marys went to embalm the

body. But the blessing for which the ages longed broke upon them that glorious dawn: His body was not there.

Yet somehow He was there with recognizable face and familiar hair, with the same scarred hands, vividly demonstrated in ways no heartbroken writers could have conceived of fabricating.

He first reappeared to a former prostitute. Could you have imagined that, or that He would cook breakfast or go fishing? He forced the clenched fist of Thomas into His death wound, and in the most dazzling combination of moves, He convinced those masters of skepticism, the Apostles, that He had not only risen but that He would never leave them desolate.

He was so full of Himself, so thoroughly victor over our last enemy, death, that here we are, almost two thousand years later, confident that He will not only shine the light of the world on us, but will stay with us until all the string is wound.

Notes:

1. William Whiston, trans., *The Works of Flavius Josephus* (New York: Holt, Reinhart & Winston, Inc., no date, orig. pub. 1890), p. 548.

2. Tacitus, Suetonius, and Pliny. *See* Will Durant, *Caesar and Christ: A History of Roman Civilization From Its Beginnings To A.D. 337* (New York: Simon & Schuster, 1944).

3. Durant, *Caesar and Christ*, p. 558.

4. Edgar J. Goodspeed, *A Life of Jesus* (New York: Harper & Bros., 1968), pp. 33, 34.

6

Jesus' Most Famous Travel Tip

"*A* certain man went down from Jerusalem to Jericho . . ." and so begins that most famous of all the stories Jesus ever told. It was not only about a traveler, it was told to a traveler. And it gives the best tip we have to find that far distant city we all seek. The story suggests that the secret is not simply at the end of the Golden String but develops enroute. This is one of the hints in the Bible that jumps out for special emphasis.

This story of the Good Samaritan sheds unexpected light on our journey, not only down the road but into the ditches on both sides. Actually "the certain man" represents us, and the dangerous thief-infested road he went "down" is ours, too.

Thank God a bold legal mind had the nerve to blurt out our dilemma to Christ: "How do we get there?" The lawyer was not tempting Christ to sin, as one reading of the King James might suggest, but trying to test Christ's thoroughness, and to get this crucial issue straight since he had Christ's full attention. The lawyer phrased it: "Master, what shall I do to inherit eternal life?" (Luke 10:25.)

What a break for this book that we have Jesus' answer. Jesus characteristically first asked the lawyer what he thought about the best route. "What is written in the law? how readest thou?" Jesus knew He was discussing this with one of Abraham's sons, so He wasn't starting from scratch, but Jesus must have been literally floored when this good Jew came back with the most important answer which Jesus Himself came up with when the lawyer grilled him in Matthew 22:36.

Jesus not only pronounced the answer right, He explained that it was *the* answer. "Do this and you shall *live*" (Luke 10:28, *italics mine*). Christ told the lawyer in Matthew that the whole Bible hung from His shining answer: "On these two commandments hang all the law and the prophets" (Matthew 22:40). That is about as helpful a travel tip as we'll ever have.

Then the lawyer "willing to justify himself" said unto Jesus, "And who is my neighbour?" Critics often put this lawyer down for trying to make himself look good with this seemingly unimportant appendix. Not at all. This lawyer has mapped out the solution to our spiritual geography.

For this second question of our lawyer drew from Christ His most beloved story. Thank God our beloved physician put it down, for apparently Matthew and Mark forgot. If a person knows only one of Christ's stories, this is it. We have that lawyer to thank for not letting Christ get away without the shortcut this answer brings us along the Golden String.

"A certain man went down from Jerusalem to Jericho." Technically this is a story of how to get out of Jerusalem instead of how to get in, but the story is definitely told to get us out of the earthly Jerusalem and into the heavenly one.

"A certain man went down from Jerusalem to Jericho, and he fell. . . ." My esteemed colleague, Dr. Browning Ware, stops the story at this point, because this is precisely what happens to all travelers on earth. Sooner or later we fall as did creation itself, which occasioned our trip to begin with. Jesus' story really is taking into account our original shipwreck which we acknowledged in chapter 2, but the pursuit of the Golden String also involves a near disaster. There is a casualty on the highway.

Though we are fortified with Christ's counsel, that does not turn our expedition into a Sunday school picnic. We must be prepared for this excursion with more than a spare tire and a jack. A shadow hangs over the journey. A bumper sticker reads: "Just because you're paranoid doesn't mean someone's *not* out to get you."

We must fight the temptation to fear that we are doomed, but there are some negatives, requiring precautions. And one of the most important is to heed Christ's comments about a basket case.

This "certain man" fell immediately into uncertainty,

specifically "among thieves," for that stretch of road was notorious for crime. Jericho was a rich plum to pick. Marc Antony on one occasion had plucked Jericho for Cleopatra, but the familiar crime was to work over depositors entering or leaving the bank of Jericho.

This particular band of brigands really roughed up their victim, "leaving him half dead." Jesus was not pulling any punches with the lawyer. That's life for anybody caught on earth. The Golden String goes through the valley of the shadow, seemingly on the rebound from Jerusalem.

"And by chance there came down a certain priest." What luck for that casualty. The poor man was no sooner down and out, and there was a preacher on the way. What more could a needy fellow want? For it might just as easily have been another crook who would have finished him off in retaliation for having nothing left. Wouldn't it be just like Jesus to cast a religious person as the hero, as in *Ben Hur*, or a nice Sunday school pageant? That would only be smart, too, for the religious people were in power then and could get you a good deal in sacrificial lambs if you treated them right—or have your water turned off if you didn't.

Jesus' clergyman in this story was a shock. Instead of running to the rescue, shouting "this is right in my line," "when he saw him, he passed by on the other side." To make the preacher the villain still shakes us, but that would also be considered both anti-Semitic and unpatriotic back then. Jesus' breaking the Sabbath and braving Pharisees was bad enough, but blasting the religious establishment broadside was suicide. It certainly was no way to get elected Messiah.

As if that were not enough, the plot of the story darkens with the arrival of the next passerby. He, too, was a religious type, a Levite, a member of the group assigned to assist the temple priests. And it is interesting that Jesus does not have the two traveling together. The assistant to the preacher is eating the other's dust, which does not, however, arouse his sympathy for the poor fellow lying in the dust.

Already Jesus has conveyed volumes in this tiny vignette. The professional religious people not only have no monopoly on God, they may be farthest from Him, as they travel far from one another. The secret of the Golden String has less to do with attendance at religious services than with one's behavior on a lonely road at night when nobody is looking.

The tragedy in Jesus' story is not so much in the thieves' attack as it is in the clergy's indifference to it. Nothing those two pious scoundrels could do when they got to Jericho could ever make up for their glaring omission enroute. The priest and Levite fell among interior thieves far more fierce. An investigator of that crime might not have found any external bruises on them, but they were more deeply wounded. Their hearts and minds took the beating that had bloodied the first victim.

It says "the travelers went *down* from Jerusalem," to Jericho. Nothing could be lower down than what those two did not do. Perhaps they feared the casualty would contaminate them or was bait for an ambush. Good reasons would occur to such defensive drivers.

Jesus' audience must have been stunned by the way He told on these powers that be, for He was portraying them as religious types who could never lead you into Jericho. Such stereotypes were blind guides to any eternal city. No one will ever get anywhere in life following them. Jesus is using these two characters to demonstrate that *how* you get there determines whether you do. Gandhi said, "The means *are* the end at an incipient stage." Christians do not believe that the end ever justifies the means. When the fast lane we're living in, with its crammed flight schedules and tight appointments, distracts us from "the way," then no matter what good time we're making and how punctual we are, we've lost strategic ground going in the wrong direction. We've lost our way; we've broken the Golden String.

Once a flight attendant came by to ask me, "What is your ultimate destination?" while I had my mouth full. Momentarily realizing what an enormously probing question that really was, I rolled my eyes heavenward. She joined me in laughing off the usual "Jericho" answers, sensing that far more important journey that engages us.

To get back to Jesus' story, the third traveler finally comes by the stricken form. It is a moment of great dramatic intensity, for the two guys who were supposed to help were flops. So while someone has no doubt run off to tattle to the authorities about this country Carpenter's disturbance of the peace, certainly the audience is tensed for what's next. But they were hardly prepared for the third man.

But a certain Samaritan, as he journeyed, came where he was: and when he saw him, he had compassion on him, and went to him, and bound up his wounds, pouring in oil and wine, and set him on his own beast, and brought him to an inn, and took care of him. And on the morrow when he departed, he took out two pence, and gave them to the host, and said unto him, Take care of him; and whatsoever thou spendest more, when I come again, I will repay thee.

Luke 10:33–35

If the audience of this tiny literary scene had been blown away by the clergy cast as villains, they must have gone into a rage over a Samaritan as the hero. To Jesus' audience a Samaritan was a total loss. His people had violated an unforgivable sacred taboo by worshiping at a forbidden shrine, and so all Samaritans were branded with this despicable heresy, making them almost as untouchable as lepers. The only good Samaritan was a dead one. Law-abiding Jews would have been revolted by Jesus' starring such a wretch in the story. Jesus' Cross was being built from infractions such as this.

By this time one would have thought that any reputable lawyer would have been so appalled for being caught in such a disgusting exchange that he would have vanished, or become hostile. But this one stood by Jesus and was obviously up to Jesus' final question:

> Which now of these three, thinkest thou, was neighbour unto him that fell among thieves? And he said, He that shewed mercy on him. Then said Jesus unto him, Go, and do thou likewise.
>
> Luke 10:36, 37

For all we know this lawyer nerved Christ to tell this story. Whatever, Jesus found one good Jew who acknowledged the comedy of his own people and one Samaritan's moral superiority. This lawyer would go down in history for giving Jesus the great commandment, and for drawing Jesus' best story out of Him. Some lawyer. Some exchange.

The Samaritan did not do the least he could get away with: notify the police, or leave a splash of wine in a dished out rock nearby. "He poured oil and wine." He gave up his ride for the half-dead fellow. He not only put the victim up for the night, but also one has the impression he stayed up with him. And the next morning he arranged for his patient to convalesce at the inn until he was well enough to leave. Jesus' Samaritan knew how to show up two reverends. The enormous contribution of the Samaritan, of course, was that "he had compassion."

The Samaritan also knew when to quit, how to take the innkeeper in on it. He did not take his fellow traveler with him to be his pet charity or permanent parasite. He was interested in getting him back on his feet, not in creating a liability. When the self-righteous judge in *The Fall*, by Albert Camus, saw a blind man standing on a street corner, he would snatch a hand away from any solicitude but his. The Samaritan was not a show-off and not after a reward. He left the next morning before the victim was able to thank him.

Isn't it remarkable that the Samaritan never questioned whether the casualty would be better off dead? He went all out to save the man's life. Christians today find themselves on all sides of the techniques, but surely Jesus meant we must always hold life precious, always revere life, and do our best to counteract those who would destroy it. This does not mean that there are not many shadings. Whose life are we revering: the mother's, the child's, or another's? Life and breath are not the same thing, and we cannot despise the life of those who disagree with us as to the will of God in a specific instance. My physician father-in-law, who was strictly prolife and in opposition to abortion except when the mother's life was endangered, nonetheless absolutely opposed what he called "heroics" as his own aged life neared its end. He wanted no medical interference with what he believed was his natural death, or perhaps I should say his supernatural transition to the life that would not die. So there are many paradoxical aspects to the increasingly complex challenge of birth and death.

It is as though the Old Testament statement ". . . I have set before you life and death. . . . choose life. . ." (Deuteronomy 30:19) has exploded with new meaning in our time. Jesus' Good Samaritan was obviously faithful to this trust as we must be.

A physician recently asked a colleague whether he would recommend an abortion in the case of a pregnant woman who had, as I remember it, TB and whose husband had syphilis. They were also very poor and they already had twelve children, two of whom were handicapped and two retarded. The colleague replied quickly, "I would terminate the pregnancy, of course." "Then," said the questioner, "you would have killed Beethoven!"

George Plagenz, the distinguished religion columnist for the *Columbus Citizen Journal,* wrote in his column for September 6, 1985, in answer to a question he had recently been given while playing a game called Scruples:

"You are a doctor. A baby is born with an incurable disorder and is in extreme pain. Do you prescribe an overdose?"

I am impressed by some of the arguments of euthanasia advocates, especially as they apply to older people. Life and breath are not the same. You don't necessarily give life by giving breath. Can we call something life that has neither usefulness nor hope of happiness?

While I was thinking of what my answer should be, I recalled the story of the young doctor who was called to deliver a baby into a poverty-stricken family in Montana.

The child had one cruelly deformed leg and was having difficulty breathing.

"The other children will call him 'Limpy'," the doctor thought. "His life will be miserable. If I don't do anything for his breathing, he will die. Wouldn't that be better?"

Then he remembered his Hippocratic oath. He began blowing into the baby's mouth until the lungs were acting normally and the child gave its first cry.

Years later the doctor's daughter and her husband were killed in an auto accident. The doctor took in their ten-year-old daughter—his grandchild—to bring up. One day a mysterious malady struck the child. It looked like polio.

The best clinics determined it was not polio, but a similar and incurable condition. The girl would be helpless for life.

The doctor learned there was a young doctor in the Midwest who had been getting excellent results in the treatment of this particular disease. He took his grandchild to see the doctor.

The young physician was lame. The older doctor's mind went back 35 years to that moment when he had delivered a crippled boy in Montana. Could it be?

It was!

Comparing notes, they found he was indeed the deformed baby into whose mouth the older doctor had breathed 35 years before. Because of his own infirmity, the young doctor had specialized in this crippling disease.

The treatment on the older doctor's grandchild was successful and the little girl was returned to normal health.

I read the question on my Scruples card a second time. Now there was no doubt what my answer would be.

The remarkable feature of the Samaritan's compassion is his availability. Gabriel Marcel honored availability as the most precious quality of love, and it is most in jeopardy today. Most of us exalt love on paper, in sermons and discussions. But the Samaritan was capable of unpremeditated mercy. He helped the ditched traveler when he was not budgeted for it, and when the man had made no appointment with him. The Samaritan had love left over from his other engagements. His schedule allowed love for the unexpected nobody who fell between the cracks. The Samaritan was not so preoccupied, not so tied up, not so packaged, as our next chapter puts it, that he could not drop everything and run to someone groaning along a lonely road.

What a story for our piece-of-string theme: four travelers. I have found myself identifying with each one of them. For instance, I am a priest and I have no trouble at all seeing myself, as Camus confesses, rushing over a bridge at night, successfully convincing myself that that was not a cry I heard from the cold water below! And how many times have I reassured myself, like the Levite, that since the preacher ahead of me didn't risk it, I won't either.

Of course, it is easy for me to fantasize myself as a Good Samaritan, always at the ready, but when I try to recollect evidence of it, either people know enough not to call on me or I'm going along so blindly I forget to notice how full the ditches are. I wish that I were the kind of person, like the Samaritan, who did such things, all in a day's work, and quickly forgot them. But even at my most arrogant I have the sneaking suspicion that heaven is not peopled with my debtors impatient to sing my praises for hosts of "little unremembered acts of kindness and of love."

Then there are times when I feel as though I'm the

fellow who fell among the thieves; having been fleeced and left, here I am half-dead, like the toothless old man I know who tells anyone who will listen about the way his wife divorced him. He pauses from his digging, shoves his hat back, looks off into the distance and sighs, "She took me for everything I had."

Look what life has done to some of us all the time, and all of us some of the time. The greedy vultures have picked our bones clean. I need help. I need a nurse. Even our Republican president entering surgery jauntily said to his physicians, "I hope you fellows are Republicans."

Worst of all, I see myself among the thieves, greedily looking upon innocent passersby as "contacts" to be made. If I'm not living off the government, I'm living off my father's legacy, or a big bundle that our company won in not the nicest cutthroat competition. Haven't I ever thought about someone *I wish you were dead?* I fear those thieves might recognize me as one of them. Who will I work over tonight to get what I want?

This story shows that Jesus is not interested in what others think of us, so He never reads obituaries. He wants to know all about what happened to you when you were alone that night on that lonely stretch of road.

"How do I get to heaven?" Ever afterward the lawyer who asked that question would see a despised Samaritan kneeling by someone who had fallen. And right beside him surely he would perceive a piece of string glowing in the gathering darkness.

7

Thy Word
Is a
Light Upon
My Path

The Golden String is not simply the feat of Abraham and Moses, or of our following just anyone's version of Christ, no matter how honestly. It involves our following the whole counsel of God as it has been provided for us in the Bible. The Bible guides us like a Golden String. "Thy word is a lamp unto my feet."

Aleksandr I. Solzhenitsyn's semi-autobiographical story, *One Day in the Life of Ivan Denisovich,* demonstrates the unbelievable power our beloved Book still has. Ivan notices that one of his fellow prisoners in the Gulag Archipelago is not broken, and the light in his eyes does not go out, as it seems to in all the other convicts. This is because each night in his bunk before the glimmering bulb is turned off, this man reverently unfolds some wrinkled pieces of paper that have somehow escaped the censor. On them are copied passages from the Gospels. The Book of Life was the secret of this man's route deep in the darkest corner behind the Iron Curtain.

Even road signs are erected to remind us to search the Scriptures, but Bible study has plunged us into such bitter disputes that the Supreme Court decided to call time-out during school. A pope might say, "I told you so." The Book of Romans no sooner saved Martin Luther than he tossed the Book of Revelation into the appendix of his German translation. Luther's Bible study split the church in two. Henry VIII strangled and burned William Tyndale, the Father of the English Bible, for daring to translate God's Holy Word into the vulgar tongue.

When the King James Version was published in 1611, thousands of copies were sunk in the Thames. Even copies of the Revised Standard Version were burned when it appeared in the 1950s, though the RSV states in its preface, "In the Bible we have not merely an historical document and a classic of English literature, but the Word of God."

Bible study has at times brought out the worst in us as well as the best. The Middle East is not the only place that is still stinging over the fighting words and wars people have suffered over this Book. The Bible is the half-hidden issue now between the West and behind the Iron Curtain. It is a sore point between the Ivy League Schools and the Bible Belt.

As a boy back in Missouri, Mark Twain remembered when the town drunk was dying in the street. Someone opened a big Bible and cruelly laid it on the old man's chest. It hastened his death. Men still throw the Book at one another like that. The Bible can inflame brilliant liberal and conservative students into self-righteous prigs or fanatics. Jesus was killed by spiritual experts who knew their Bible cold, but knew not the Spirit and ". . . weightier matters of the law . . ." (Matthew 23:23).

Many American families have reacted so negatively against their Puritanical backgrounds that their children now have overreacted against their disbelief. Generations flip back and forth.

Others had come to believe that the King James Version was not only "the Word of God," but the very words of God. But by the time this century was under way, college religion courses were pointing out a printer's error in the King James: "strain at a gnat" (Matthew 23:24) instead of *out*. This mistake is still evident in some old editions of the King James Version. Furthermore, hundreds of English words no longer said to the reader what their translators meant them to say. For instance, "suffer little children . . . to come unto me . . ." meant in King James' time, "let little children come to me" (Matthew 19:14).

Even more shocking were the questions scholars brought up in the Bible study that came to be known as higher criticism. As a child, Albert Schweitzer had dared to ask, "How could Jesus have been poor after all His birthday gifts of gold, frankincense, and myrrh?" Others asked such questions as, "How could Moses have written the Pentateuch since it includes the account of the death of Moses?" Still others had the nerve to ask, "How could

Isaiah be one book since there is an obvious gap of centuries between the end of chapter thirty-nine and the beginning of chapter forty?"

Many of our forebears lost their faith, and many of us have kept hands off the Bible, because of these bewildering developments in Bible study.

I took the most liberal position to begin my ministry, partly to avoid the general disillusionment that had fallen on many biblical literalists. But I have come to realize that our Bible-believing forebears may not have been as foolish as we are.

Bible study is not strictly an intellectual pursuit; it is an extremely personal matter. A distinguished nuclear physicist enlightened me that such matters as our belief in God, or the Bible, involve an act of will even more than our minds. While we are commanded to love God with "all thy mind," our little minds are the tools of our strong wills. Our minds are the willing slaves of what we want in our hearts. We never take a purely rational or objective position, particularly on such matters as Mother and God. We summon our minds to support our preferences and prejudices. God is someone we fall in love with, or don't. Then we proceed to justify it all intellectually. "There is no uninterpreted data."

While we worship God, we study the Bible. We must not become bibliolatrists, so we must not be afraid to ask questions. Furthermore, the Bible is more a miracle of art than it is a military map or a mathematical equation. For instance, Jesus spoke not with theological precision but as a poet. He used parables, paradoxes, and Oriental hyperboles employing amusing exaggeration, and, often, the most puzzling questions. What He said says different things to people at different times. C. S. Lewis wrote in his *Reflections on the Psalms:*

> Taken by a literalist Jesus will always prove the most elusive of teachers. Systems cannot keep up with that darting illumination. No net less wide than a man's whole heart, nor less fine of mesh than love, will hold the sacred fish.

The Bible commands us, for instance, to celebrate the Passover: "And ye shall observe this thing for an ordinance to thee and to thy sons for ever" (Exodus 12:24). Completed Jewish Christians take this literally, while many other supposed literalists do not. No command in the Bible could be clearer than the one that proclaims the Year of Jubilee: "And ye shall hallow the fiftieth year, and proclaim liberty throughout all the land . . . it shall be a jubile unto you . . ." (Leviticus 25:10). However, few Christians take these words literally, any more than they do the commands in Leviticus to follow kosher diet and circumcision which the New Testament explicitly cancels.

By the turn of the century, Bible study included scholars reckless enough to suspect that Jesus had never actually lived. Then Albert Schweitzer undertook to prove that Jesus was suffering from pathological delusions. Instead, Schweitzer's research convinced him that Jesus was not only a vivid historic figure, but that, as we noted earlier, "The Gospel of Mark, in essentials, is genuine history." Schweitzer entitled his conclusions *The Quest for the Historical Jesus,* and that volume became the milestone beginning the modern certification of the Bible in terms that an honest atheist could not deny.

Schweitzer himself finally took the Bible so seriously

that he gave up all his academic degrees and distinguished posts and went to Africa to serve as a missionary physician. For he read Jesus' story of the rich man and Lazarus. So when his patients awakened from the anesthetic the first words they heard were the old doctor's, "The reason you have no more pain is because the Lord Jesus told me to come to the banks of the Ogowe." That's what the Bible did to one higher critic.

While we must maintain room for all kinds of temperaments and approaches to the Bible, and while there will always be textual problems and unanswerable questions, such as whether the stories of Job and Jonah are biographical or parabolic, we are discovering more and more how incredibly accurate the Bible is.

The copy of Isaiah found in the Dead Sea Scrolls was dated by carbon radioactive test to be a thousand years older than any other known copy of Isaiah. It matched our more recent manuscripts except for one or two words. Not only has the Bible been copied reliably, the original copy was reliable. The late Nelson Glueck, world-renowned Jewish archaeologist, insisted that his phenomenal success in unearthing ancient cities was because he dug for them where the Bible located them.

Good Bible study not only permits but encourages varying if not conflicting interpretations. One derives deeper, and sometimes different, meanings each time through the same passage. The Bible, however, is not simply a study Book. The Bible is a holy Book. And so, as even Mark Twain said, "What bothers me most about the Bible is what I *do* understand." It is a miracle filled with miracles that can happen to the reader now.

Often the professor who knows the Bible academically

misses the point of it. Then some uneducated John Bunyan picks up the Bible as a child might and it falls open to the page and verse that transforms him. His mind may not have been prepared, but neither were his defenses prepared. His heart was ready.

This impromptu scenario has happened many times, humbling our proud pretensions to respectable Bible study. It happened to Saint Augustine himself, who was probably the most famous and the most influential student of the Bible who ever lived. He had been a renowned professor of rhetoric in the last days of Rome and, according to his *Confessions*, one of the most depraved profligates who ever lived. One day while he was sitting in a garden he heard a child singing, "Take up and read." He turned to the Book beside him and read the verse that revolutionized his life, ". . . not in rioting and drunkenness, not in chambering and wantonness, not in strife and envying. But put ye on the Lord Jesus Christ . . ." (Romans 13:13, 14).

That kind of thing still happens. Some study the Bible for years without its overpowering them; for others, one glance is enough to completely change their lives. A contemporary Christian entertainer had formerly been a priest of Satan in a church of two thousand members. He traced his moment of truth to just such an Augustinian introduction to the Word of God.

He had literally floored a Christian with his fists for bothering him with the Bible. After they had removed the bleeding martyr, the atheist noticed that his missionary's Bible had been left behind open to John 3:16: "For God so loved the world, that he gave his only begotten Son, that whosoever believeth in him should not perish, but have everlasting life." It took only one word in that passage to knock him out of Satan's pulpit and into Christ's. It was that loving word *whosoever*. He identified with that word. He was a *whosoever*.

Obviously there is more to Bible study than this "let the Bible fall open by itself" method. One man's finger fell on the words, "and Judas went out and hanged himself." He tried again and he found himself reading, "Go thou and do likewise." He opened the Bible one more time and it told him, "What thou must do, do quickly."

But this most primitive form of Bible study does point out that there is much more to the Bible than Bible study. For however long it takes to find oneself in it, the Bible truly is a mirror. And while, as Kierkegaard suggests, it is permissible to count its cracks, measure, and date it, the idea is to find oneself in the Bible—and not allow study of the mirror to distract us from our self-discovery. Rembrandt's remarkable studies of the Bible are well-known, but not everyone realizes that he caught and painted himself red-handed in the mob scene at the Crucifixion.

So, according to Kierkegaard, when one reads in the story of the Good Samaritan that a priest went by on the other side of the road from the "man who fell among thieves," don't say it was a priest. Since the Bible is a mirror, say, "It was I." And so with the Levite. Then when the good Samaritan comes by and helps, so one won't get bored always saying, "I," say, "That was not I."

The Bible is not only a mirror, it is also a love letter from God. So we read it not only as students, not finally even as pilgrims, but as loved ones, hanging on His next word.

Perhaps the next step is to get a Bible. The family Bible lying around the house is probably the King James Version; though now updated, it was originally translated from Hebrew and Greek into English in 1611. It is still the unparalleled masterpiece of English literature. The forty learned men who translated it were masters of the English as well as of the ancient tongues. In those Elizabethan times one had to be competent enough in English to write a sonnet in order to win a lady's hand in marriage.

While most of the new translations are superior technically, sometimes their English is flat in comparison to the King James. Many more ancient manuscripts are available to today's translators, so the translations may be more accurate, and in many instances are much clearer with archaic language removed, but their English does not equal the King James.

Here is an example of what I mean by the surpassing beauty of the King's English in the King James Version. In Genesis 6:5, 6 God is pondering how far His creation has fallen:

> And God saw that the wickedness of man was great in the earth, and that every imagination of the thoughts of his heart was only evil continually.
> And it repented the Lord that he had made man on the earth, and it grieved him at his heart.

So we must keep the King James and add to it the New English Bible and perhaps the very excellent and readable paraphrase by J. B. Phillips. One also needs a good commentary, perhaps Barclay's or the more extensive Interpreter's Bible. One should also have access to a concordance and a dictionary of the Bible.

Armed and familiar with these tools, where does one begin? Probably not with Genesis, although millions have read the Bible from cover to cover before they knew "better." Those who constructed the Canon must have had some such study design in mind. And numerous readers have not only survived but been inspired by several such marathons. One of the great biblical scholars of modern times read the New Testament through in one sitting each Easter eve.

While studying the Bible with and under others is recommended, much is to be said for studying it alone. It may not be possible for most of us to grab a copy and head for the hills, but the Good Book opens some of its treasures only to the one who ponders it heavily in secret. The verses of Holy Scripture leaped to the lips of Christ during His forty days and nights alone. It is good to remember in this day of cram courses and speed-reading programs that God does not perform well in an accelerated program. One can take the Bible for credit and completely miss the reward that only comes to someone who can stay at home and sit still with the Bible in his lap.

It was in this light that one saint was led to suggest that the study of the Bible might well begin with the private reading of the Book of 1 John each night for a month.

Others have preferred to approach the Bible topically as is done by a number of patented procedures. By using the concordance anyone could also compose his own topical study such as systematically selecting all the references under *hope*, or *love*, or *the Kingdom of God*. Illustrious friends I know are excited by their study of the Bible through its personalities, spending one week on Abraham, one on Moses, and so on.

My preference would be to have you find the teacher God has sent you and begin with the Gospel of Mark, usually considered to be the first Gospel written. You will discover that Mark got his material mostly from Peter who is prominent in that Gospel. You will soon wonder why Matthew is so similar to Mark but with more detail. Scholars call this the synoptic problem.

Did Matthew place first in the New Testament and have more copious notes because he actually was Levi, Jesus' literate tax-collector secretary? Goodspeed and others call attention to the preponderance of statistics and far higher register of figures in Matthew which confirm an accountant's style.

The record number of healings and medical details distinguish Luke for the physician's book it is, as well as his sequel, Acts. Luke gallantly introduces more women and appreciates more poor than the other Gospels.

Key questions can assist the student of the Bible to plumb the depths of each book or passage:

1. What questions do I have?
2. What is unique?
3. To whom is the author writing?
4. What difference will this make in my life?

Before I conclude with a passage in the Bible that illustrates good Bible study and might serve as a point of departure for any group about to begin Bible study, let me mention one peril.

Not long ago I saw the great cathedral of Chartres in France rising in the distance before me. It is one of the most awesome sights in all the world. I could readily understand how, upon seeing it from afar, pilgrims would immediately fall on their knees in penitence and adoration, then crawl the rest of the way to this holy place.

As I entered those majestic doors of the House of God, I could scarcely speak and wanted to weep alone. Instead, the cathedral was filled with the discordance of guides, some with loudspeakers, jabbering about the height of the spires and where the stone for the building had been quarried. Without realizing what they were doing, the guides had taken the cathedral away from us, in order to give us their talk on it.

This is the peril of Bible study. The glory of the Book can be taken away in exchange for some study guide insights and statistics. Most of us have only a moment of a lifetime to see and feel Chartres. So it is with the Bible. Here we are in the presence of Luke, that glorious and beloved physician, and if we don't watch out someone will have taken Luke from us in return for pedantic data. "Have you *done* Luke?" Oh God, what *have* we done to Luke? Tragically, one course in Shakespeare can "kill" Shakespeare for someone.

Hopefully your teacher will not be simply informed but aware. How fortunate you are if she is humble enough to let you teach her. The true lover of nature who leads little children on a nature walk will allow time for the wonder of the woods to cause a shiver or two of ecstasy. He will not swallow up the sunset with his words, nor disdain the silence into which the Word of God was first spoken to those who took it down for us to study. It is far more important to delight in a maple than to be able to identify it. What if only one verse were read at Bible study and no one was allowed to speak, or prattle, for an hour?

I have decided to protect you from comments I might make about this concluding keepsake. It is taken from the twenty-sixth to the thirty-ninth verses of the eighth chapter of Acts according to the King James Version. I offer it as an illustration of how it showed a traveler the way to go.

And the angel of the Lord spake unto Philip, saying, Arise, and go toward the south unto the way that goeth down from Jerusalem unto Gaza, which is desert.

And he arose and went: and, behold, a man of Ethiopia, an eunuch of great authority under Candace queen of the Ethiopians, who had the charge of all her treasure, and had come to Jerusalem for to worship,

Was returning, and sitting in his chariot read Esaias the prophet.

Then the Spirit said unto Philip, Go near, and join thyself to this chariot.

And Philip ran thither to him, and heard him read the prophet Esaias, and said, Understandest thou what thou readest?

And he said, How can I, except some man should guide me? And he desired Philip that he would come up and sit with him.

The place of the scripture which he read was this, He was led as a sheep to the slaughter; and like a lamb dumb before his shearer, so opened he not his mouth:

In his humiliation his judgment was taken away: and who shall declare his generation? for his life is taken from the earth.

And the eunuch answered Philip, and said, I pray thee, of whom speaketh the prophet this? of himself, or of some other man?

Then Philip opened his mouth, and began at the same scripture, and preached unto him Jesus.

And as they went on their way, they came unto a certain water: and the eunuch said, See, here is water; what doth hinder me to be baptized?

And Philip said, If thou believest with all thine heart,

thou mayest. And he answered and said, I believe that
Jesus Christ is the Son of God.

And he commanded the chariot to stand still: and they
went down both into the water, both Philip and the
eunuch; and he baptized him.

And when they were come up out of the water, the
Spirit of the Lord caught away Philip, that the eunuch saw
him no more: and he went on his way rejoicing.

PART II

FORKS
IN
THE
ROAD

8

The Chief Obstacle

The chief obstacle to our picking up the threads and following the Lord Jesus is dishonesty. "The truth will make you free." Falsehood is the warden of our hell. We superficially assume honesty to be the kindergarten of faith. No. Honesty may be the topmost step up the ladder of sainthood. If the Bible is our starting point, the first fork we run into is dishonesty. Nothing disables us or disrupts our journey like dishonesty. You can't be honest and disbelieve in God. Tolstoy wrote:

> The only significance of life consists in helping to establish the Kingdom of God, and this can be done only by means of the acknowledgement of the truth by each one of us.

Who me? Yes. The nearest example of our deceit lies in our typical greeting. "How are you?" "I am fine." Far be it from me to encourage hypochondriacs to drag us through their operations again, but the usual, "I'm fine," as brave and brief as it may be, denies the truth at the outset of our communication. We paint on a smile, skirt the real issue with lame observations about the weather, then trot out our trophies: "Our youngest got a Rhodes Scholarship." Or we grill the other person before they grill us, all the time trying to hide the blue mark on our cheek. But if they ask about it, we're ready with a good story to camouflage our falling down the stairs after three drinks on an empty stomach—which we took to assuage our bitter loneliness.

Our problems, of course, are not really the business of just any passing acquaintance. But our reserve, which is proper there, easily makes a wider sweep until before we know it we're two- or three-faced people, as unreal to our friends as to innocent bystanders. We are soon bent out of shape by a world lubricated by dishonesty. One might expect a lot of bull at the cocktail party, but it is just as bountiful in school and at church.

A deceitful child is usually the result of poor parenting, perhaps from too little or too much pressure. However, the most honest child inevitably emerges from adolescence with secrets vital to his maturation; but it is difficult to restrict it to necessity. Little white lies seem a necessary defense against stronger people invading our privacy and robbing us of our rights, but this acceptable practice easily entails a tangled web of deception that destroys integrity and distracts us from the Golden String.

For instance, someone inquires, "What are you doing?" Obviously we ought not to have to tell him that we are treating ourself for acne or have just had an interview with our probation officer; but such justifiable discretion quickly grows into our making up stuff until we have completely forgotten Christ's caution: "Let what you say be simply 'Yes' or 'No' . . ." (Matthew 5:37 RSV).

Stephen Leacock made fun of a young curate whom he called Melpomenus Jones. That young minister's cowardly honesty cut off every avenue of retreat from his first pastoral call. His honesty locked him in that visit until death kindly came and rescued him. The young Reverend Jones's call went smoothly at first. He drank a cup of tea and leafed through the family photograph album. After an hour or so he rose to say, "I must be going now." His hostess asked, "Must you go so soon?" Being honest about his vacation starting the next day he confessed that he really did not have to leave. So he drank more tea and leafed through their album once more. Repeatedly he rose to go and repeatedly his hostess put him through the same routine.

Finally the husband came home from work; they all had dinner together, and it got to be quite late. At last the frantic husband teased, "Couldn't you stay all night?" To be perfectly honest, there was no reason why he couldn't. The days passed until, bloated with tea and bored to death with that album, Jones became ill. He got worse and finally the day came when he could say in all honesty, "Now I really must be going," and his soul departed this life like a frightened cat shooting across a backyard fence. Honesty does not require transparency.

The issue of honesty has its serious side. Dishonesty is bad for your health, and it is as common in the hospital as it is on the way there. The sickroom is thick with false hope. Job's comforters were as filled with reproach as contemporary ones are with snow jobs. Both are about as unnerving as flattery. Such sweet talk actually isolates the patient and makes him anxious. Dishonesty becomes an unconscious habit for the patient as well as for his visitors and medical team.

I remember a very intelligent young woman who had been hospitalized for a malignancy. Her once fair complexion had become yellow as parchment and was stretched tightly over her skeletal frame, showing unmistakably that she was at the door of death. Her husband and I were anxious to break through the illusion of physical well-being in which she had wrapped herself. She was positively giddy about being sprung from bed soon; her conversation no more relating to where she was than the banal small talk to which I had made my substantial contribution over coffee.

Her husband and I decided that he would suggest I say grace next time her tray arrived, as a way of introducing God into the situation. She laughed it off—"You crazy guys think of everything"—and dawdled over her food with more inane dialogue. She absolutely refused to level with her husband and minister, even in the face of disaster. Dishonesty makes life and death unreal, and therefore unrewarding.

Don't think deceiving ourselves is so rare. I've done practically the same thing as that young woman. Some years ago I had a recurring symptom that I repeatedly brushed aside without mentioning. Had I known of anyone else having this symptom I would have insisted they have immediate medical attention. But when it threatened me I was able to dismiss it as though I assumed things like that don't happen to me. I was like the man who explained his attitude toward death by saying, "I have always thought that an exception would be made in my case." We are able to blind ourselves to anything we do not want to believe.

A wife may go to her grave telling her husband that she loves him, while they both know all along that she never did. She insisted that she did because—well, for a number of reasons: She was too proud to admit she'd made a mistake to the many eager to tell her, "I told you so." She also felt sorry for him. She felt guilty, cornered; besides, what would people think? How many people kid themselves?

"Do you like me?" How honest will my replies be to my boss, my rival, my teacher from whom I crave an A. I have been a teacher. I like to think I was a good one, which would indicate that I loved the subject and the students. But there were other pressing fears and foibles that jeopardized my integrity as someone who should be mainly concerned about my students learning. I found myself excessively concerned about making students manageable. I was too preoccupied with parading my knowledge. I was more concerned with doing whatever it took to keep and improve my job than I was with praying for them to fall in love with the truth.

How easily I add a little twist to the questionable gossip I hear about the president, or my colleague, as I pass it on.

I don't bother to check on the story or to minimize it. Honesty is not as juicy as derogatory tidbits, though someone else may be misquoting me. So we run back and forth to one another, manufacturing behind each other's backs these dark myths born more from wishful thinking and ill will than from facts.

Some of us suffer from inferiority. Many more of us from some sort of illusion of grandeur, which may be nearly the same thing. People try to convince themselves they did their best, like the elder brother in the parable, unable to think of anything to apologize for, or to think of any thanks. Is there any justice, to say nothing of humility? Always populating hell with others and heaven with ourselves may be arrogant, but it may also be downright dishonest. False witness makes us stumble on our path to heaven's gate. It is breaking the tenth commandment.

A few years ago a young minister I knew of in upstate New York announced his resignation to the board of elders because he had lost his faith. Official boards usually take their minister's personal trauma in stride, sometimes with more curiosity than disappointment, which might check the honesty of the clergy; but this particular board was unusual. Instead of making immediate plans for their young heretic's replacement they requested a grace period, so they could all spend a few days in prayer.

The elders reported back unanimously that they wanted their young minister to stay on. He replied, "What would I preach about?" The answer came back: "You still believe in honesty don't you?" "Yes." "Well, preach about honesty, and we'll pray that the rest of your faith returns." It did, or perhaps his faith then came to him for the first time.

Mental illness has something to do with dishonesty. Some truth is too painful to look at. But our depression— or anxiety—could have something to do with burying the unbearable incident. Not until we return to the scene of the crime in our memory, not until we recall the horrible details and digest them in anger or grief will we be well. Freud was not the only one who preached: "The truth will make you free." While there are many points of view with regard to psychoanalysis, all therapy has to do with honesty.

Buried grief or anger secretly sabotage happiness. "Blessed are those who mourn. For they shall be comforted." Blessed are those who see it and say it like it is, for reality is the shortest distance to God.

Dishonesty has crawled into Christianity and distorted it from the inside far more destructively than any enemy outside. Christians blame outsiders for not coming to church, for not becoming Christians; we condemn the world wholesale for not being at peace just like those of us who pray for it and demonstrate for it with bandwagons of posters. But the trouble is that the world is just like us. Even the world is not as divided, splintered, and in conflict as many religious groups, charities, and supposedly altruistic movements.

If someone's life depended, as it does, on bringing another person to God, it would require a revolution of honesty in the evangelist's soul flowering with joy as in the story from which I shall recall called "Payment" in *The Works of Tolstoy*. Tolstoy often found and adapted such marvelous old legends.

A man who had led a wicked life repented and became godson to a hermit who assigned him the penance of watering three charred tree stumps with water brought by the mouthful from the river until they should sprout. So the godson spent half his day doing this and the other half serving the poor and keeping only the most frugal necessities for himself. Two years passed without a day missed watering the stumps mouthful by mouthful, but no sprout appeared.

One day a highwayman came by glorying in murder and robbery. The godson called upon him to repent but the robber cursed him out of the way. "Because you have reminded me of God this day, I will kill two people the more tomorrow." And the robber ridiculed the godson for living off his public piety.

The godson went on living the same for eight years, but then realized the robber was right about him. He really was being rewarded for showing off his good deeds. "I will go away into the forest—away to some new spot where the people cannot find me."

The next time the highwayman came by he asked the godson how he expected to survive since the people could not find him to leave food. "Surely God will give," the godson replied. The robber left, promising to kill the godson next time, although the hermit shouted after him to repent; that evening when the godson looked at the stumps he noticed one of them had sprouted. And when he ran out of food he found a bag of biscuits hanging on a bough. He kept finding biscuits there regularly.

One day the highwayman rode by with a prisoner he intended to torture, but the godson insisted that he let the man go, even though the robber threatened the godson with death. The godson said, "I will not let you pass . . . I fear not you, but only God." The robber let his captive go, and again the godson asked him to abandon his wicked life. The next morning the godson noticed that another stump had sprouted.

Another ten years passed before the robber reappeared. This time as the godson looked upon him he felt a great pity for him and, running to his side, clasped him by the knee: "Dear brother," he cried, "have mercy upon your own soul, for in you too dwells a God-given-spirit."

But the highway man only frowned and turned away. "Leave me," he said.

Yet the godson clasped him still closer by the knee, and burst into tears.

At that the highwayman raised his eyes and looked at the godson. He looked and looked, and then suddenly slid from his horse and threw himself upon his knees on the ground.

"Old man," he said, "you have overcome me at last. Twenty years have I striven with you, but you have gradually taken away my strength, until now I am not master of myself. Do what you will with me. The first time that you pleaded with me I was but the more enraged. It was not until you withdrew from the eyes of men and recognized that you needed not their help, that I began to think over your words. But from that moment I began to hang the bags of biscuits on the bough."

Then the godson remembered how it was only when the dirty cloth was rinsed that the table was cleansed. Even so, he saw it was only when he had ceased to take thought for himself that his heart had been purified, and he had been able to purify the hearts of others.

And the highwayman went on: "But the first real change of heart took place in me when you ceased to fear death at my hands."

Instantly the godson remembered that it was only when the felloe makers had fastened firmly the felloes block that they had been able to bend the felloes. Even so, he saw it was only when he had established firmly his life in God and humbled his presumptuous heart that he had ceased to have any fear of death. "And," said the highwayman in conclusion, "it was when your heart went out to me in pity, and you wept before me, that my own heart was changed entirely."

Rejoicing greatly, the godson led the highwayman to the spot where the three stumps were—and behold! From the third stump an apple tree had sprouted.

Then the godson remembered that it was only when the drovers' fire had kindled to a blaze that the wet brushwood had kindled with it. So also, he saw, had his heart kindled within him to a blaze, and with its flame had set fire to another.

With joy he recognized that his sins were at last redeemed.

All this he related to the highwayman and died. The highwayman laid him in his grave and lived thereafter as the godson had bidden him, and taught men to do likewise.

The godson had really allowed the robber to save him, in all honesty. Honesty saved them both, and how many more, for it is our deceit that makes the Golden String to heaven's gate disappear.

Honesty shines through Christ, brightest on the Cross. We trust He truly meant to forgive us, for He confessed, too, "I thirst." In fact, we are still shocked by His brutal frankness while hanging there, for He shouted the title of the Twenty-second Psalm which more than any other tore open the unfair agony of man blow by blow: "My God, why have You forsaken me?" He was the only One who dared to tell the whole truth and nothing but the truth that sets us free. When you are brave enough to face the facts of life, you'll see God for a fact.

9

No Package Deal

Nowadays when someone asks, "How do you get to heaven?" as the lawyer asked Jesus, we usually offer some group plan. We are "joiners," and when we jump into anything we want to organize it and regularize it with associates. After all, this is a corporate world where even the devil's got it together. We must, too: "Like a mighty army moves the church of God." So our joining the church is a proper step along the way, but we take it with a warning, for it, too, can fork.

When the lawyer asked Christ, "What do I do to inherit

eternal life?'' wouldn't you have expected Jesus to answer, "Come to Bible study," or, "I'm taking in new disciples next week." Instead He highlighted a special individual assignment.

Obviously everything involves teamwork, and no doubt a committee could have made short work of the fellow who fell among thieves, but Jesus' story told on the committee who no doubt were on their way to a well-planned meeting in Jericho on behalf of such victims. Perhaps the road was so narrow at that point there was room for only one at a time. In our pursuit of the Golden String we must go much of the way alone. The will of God is measured out to each of us, one by one. We are born alone, we die alone, and each of us must work out our own salvation alone, without expecting any church to do it for us.

Abraham did not evaluate Ur according to zones, or by social strata. The secret of Moses was not his board of trustees with its precisely trained battalions of charioteers. Jesus did not have His brothers and sisters holding His hand for forty days in the wilderness, not even in Gethsemane, nor that awful day after. He had to have it out in a private relationship with God.

So, when the lawyer inquired of Jesus about his ultimate destination, he did not end up with directions and caravan schedules. The route he was assigned had something to do with some lonely traveler giving a deserted nobody an impromptu life. Alcoholics Anonymous refers to it as the twelfth step. And old-timers are known to say, "When all else fails, twelfth-step it."

The peril of our age is to program everything. Instead of leaving someone alone to work it out with God, madden-

112

ingly detailed road maps are shoved into our hot little hands, and we are scolded about what we'd better do "or else."

Increasingly I have come to revere the Bible as the Word of God, but to pound a pulpit and attempt to dictate a peculiar worship of the Word over the worship of God is not the whole truth. Our forebears went through the most painful struggles at Plymouth to win the religious freedom we enjoy. We must not surrender this blessed privilege to agree to disagree that Roger Williams won for us. Each of us must be able to interpret Scripture according to his own private conscience, according to the light and leading of the Holy Spirit of Christ.

Liberal Christians, too, can fall into a liberalism that is as cultish as any hidebound conservative. Tragically, it is not academically safe to stand up and express belief literally in the miracle of the feeding of the five thousand at accredited divinity schools. One can encounter a subtle ridicule there that silences such "naiveté." Sometimes those environs that assume themselves to be most "enlightened" actually permit least deviation from their point of view.

As our time has taken faith less seriously, cultism has sneaked into the secular world. Take any department in a graduate school of a properly accredited university. There is a fine line between the pursuit of excellence and pathology. The reputation of a professor can depend on his department's setting almost unobtainable goals for a student. Stiff requirements for credit infringe on the students' health and sleep; they swallow up time for reflection or other normal activities that ought to be able to exist simultaneously.

When there are not hours enough in the day to accomplish the objectives the arrangement is sick. Higher learning can act so high that it becomes idolatrous and wants complete control. It tends to kill any other god by competition. You cannot worship God and education. "No man can serve two masters."

Employers as well as athletic departments and our growing bureaucracy, with its intensifying scrutiny and increasing restrictions, put the squeeze on the individual. Defected Communists have been calling attention to the encroaching censorships and erosions of the free press taking place in the free world.

Whatever wants to absorb one, body and soul, whether in the interests of efficiency or profit, is a package deal we oppose with all our hearts. The Golden String beckons us to recover the image of God defaced in us by all these demonic forces that try to box us in.

The Spirit of Christ is both a preventative and an antidote to our mania for cults. When His Spirit dwells in us we can take up golf, go into politics, or even become religious, without turning into fanatics. Saint Francis said, "Love Christ and do as you please." That didn't mean "anything goes." Someone who loves Christ, however, is as free as the air. He is not a biblical bookworm. Whether he is in church or out, he is playing it by ear, tuned not to a parental or ministerial tape, but to "the still small voice" that protects him against the network of too neat demands. These not only distract him from God, but often stick him with ground rules instead of freeing him for the person-to-person God.

I recently read a book entitled *Ice* which gives one sailor's account of his attempt to sail, alone, nearer the North Pole than anyone else had ever done. He almost made it, but he truly did find God and himself while he, his three-legged dog, and his thirty-foot craft, were frozen in an iceberg for fifteen months.

It took courage to handle that long polar night without a crew. He dressed exactly as the Eskimos recommended with chamois underwear that peeled off like skin when he finally returned. He fooled an Arctic seal into thinking he was a seal too, and fired a flare down the throat of an attacking polar bear.

That iceberg was no place for an idler. The polar sailor had his hands full just staying alive, but what I admired most was his ability to put in all that time alone, including long periods of enforced idleness, cut off from all human contact. Most of us are incapable of putting in one Sunday afternoon alone, out of the fast lane. We cannot bear life unless we are loaded with commitments and the phone is ringing off the hook, which is partly why we get hung up in cults. We don't know what to do with ourselves unless someone tells us what to do, and our mind is crammed, and our day is jammed.

God was on that ice floe; you couldn't miss Him out there. No other strident drivers hogged the road. Before that wait was over, the sailor faced fear down; he met loneliness at full force and conquered it. While we get so busy acquiring biblical data, doing the dance the church directs, we don't have time to sit and wait and listen for God to speak to us: ". . . They that wait upon the Lord shall renew their strength; they shall mount up with wings as eagles; they shall run, and not be weary; and they shall walk, and not faint" (Isaiah 40:31).

The man on the ice floe reminds me of Jesus' Samaritan. His life, too, was not paved with appointments. He was not the property of some clique. He was free to help another—free to be himself.

God is like this. Think of the father of the prodigal son Jesus told about. How different the story would be if the returning prodigal had not been observed returning or the father been too busy to take him back, too busy with the hundred and one things his "cults" had assigned to improvise something on his own.

To the contrary, when the prodigal son returned to his father he did not get a recording, nor a copy of a memo. Not too long after the son had gone, the father had apparently poised himself for the boy's return, like a runner on the starting block. At the first sight of that beloved familiar figure on the horizon the father was off and running to him, as at the sound of a gun at the beginning of a race. God is like that. Christianity is your own personal friendship with your Father in heaven for yours and your neighbors' sake through Jesus Christ our Lord.

God is not preoccupied with keeping records on us or handing out credit. He is free to listen to us, to love, and to come at anytime. Actually He is waiting for us, and as John Donne prays:

> God made sun and moon to distinguish
> Seasons and day and night
> And we cannot have the fruits of the earth
> But in their seasons, but God hath made no decree
> To distinguish the seasons of His mercies.
> In paradise the fruits were ripe the first minute
> And in heaven it is always autumn.
> His mercies are ever in their maturity.
> God never says you should have come yesterday,

He never says you must come again tomorrow but
Today, if you will hear His voice today He will
Hear you.

He brought light out of darkness
Not out of lesser light.
He can bring thy summer out of winter
Though thou have no spring.
All occasions invite His mercies
And all times are His season.

10

Battling
the
Green
Distraction

"*S*ay *thank you!*"

Those are almost the first words we learn, and they are about the last word on life. God grant, in the end, that we shall not be so distracted by the other side of the fence "where the grass is always greener," that our lives fail to flower on this side with thanksgiving. The big idea is to drown our discontent in appreciation. That attitude is what gives us altitude on our journey to the city on high. We can't make such a long trip on two legs. We need the wings only given by gratitude.

Suicide can be a way of saying "no thanks." And there are more ways to commit suicide than with pills and razor blades. You can say it with a steering wheel or with a chip on your shoulder. One can live a long time and hate every minute of it—curse God and die on your feet. Life to some people is a complaint. To others it is a front of, "I'm fine." Thanklessness makes many faces.

Before we know it we are concentrating on what is wrong with the world, as the news media means us to do, or as the red marks on our son's papers tend to do. It is so tempting to cast our eyes down, looking at the dirt. Even our prayers can depreciate God and somehow linger on the hang-ups of the persons we're praying for. This is how we lose the trail blazed by the stars.

I suspect that what turns the road away from thanks may be envy. In our consuming fear of kidnappings and collisions, we forget to warn our children of this heart-worm which burrows while they are memorizing traffic rules. Cancer and heart trouble are not the killers. Envy is. Envy devours us while we're busy taking precautions against smoking and overweight. The menace crawling invisibly through our time is not AIDS. It is envy.

Envy is how Adam and Eve went down. Instead of the first family singing out, "Isn't our orchard great?" they were absolutely mesmerized by that one and only tree that wasn't theirs. The snake sabotaged their thanksgiving with envy. He perverted their contentment in Eden, promising, "Ye shall be as gods," until they wanted what God had. They wanted His tree, His glory, for themselves. Perhaps the Fall from Eden was this pernicious desire to be in debt to no one, to be thankless. How deluded we must be not to see ourselves in their spiritual nakedness.

Battling the Green Distraction

And so the first murder was committed out of a combination of jealousy and envy. Cain could not bear the success of Abel's offering.

We like to think we have graduated to more advanced New Testament material. No, the saints who have risen above envy are few and far between. Most of us are still obsessed with the other side of the fence, with what somebody else got for Christmas. With a little more work, a little more money, a little more advance on our credit cards, we can overextend ourselves, mortgage our futures, and practically live beyond our means where the grass is greener, even though it really isn't ours, and we don't belong there.

Envy is so subtle. We would be shocked to know how cunningly we've been swallowed. Perhaps it's not a heartworm. Maybe it's a python that has coiled around us, and we're so programmed to watch for telltale signs of physical debilitation that it never occurred to us to note our eyes were turning green. "Look at that car he's driving, his new wife, that salary increase he says he's getting. And here I still am with my same old raw deal."

The stories of Adam and Eve, and Cain and Abel cut the Bible open to you and me. The "have nots" want what the "haves" have, and the "haves" want more. Webster defines *envy* as "discontent, and desire for another's qualities or identity or possessions." Next Webster adds: "malevolence, to look at with malice, to resent another's good fortune." Envy, distinguished from covetousness, would rather eliminate the person than grab what he has.

Our prisons and ghettos are not the only places packed with people pulling fast ones to compensate. Both the French and the Bolshevist Revolutions were fired up by

121

envy. But so are palaces. Kings are notoriously jealous, even of their own sons. Saul couldn't stand the women singing about David and almost speared him to the wall. David's son, Absalom, tried to steal his father's throne just as David envied Uriah because he had Bathsheba.

Envy curses the most religious life. The prodigal's elder brother was a pious creature of envy. He was a civilized Cain, so he didn't stab the prodigal; perhaps he drove him off with looks that could kill. And when the prodigal returned, the elder brother was furious with his father for throwing a feast of joy. The elder brother is the perfect example of the badhearted good men who killed Christ: ". . . it was out of envy that they had delivered him up" (Matthew 27:18 RSV).

If the elder brother could have ridden himself of envy and jealousy, here is how he might have received his little brother back:

> Dad, I beg you to take him back. I have missed him so much, and I always gave him such a hard time he had to get away and get me out of his system. He's changed, Dad. He always did have a good heart. He's not smarting over what I did to him anymore. I never told you, Dad, but I flung my good grades and sports trophies in his face. I made fun of him. I've changed, too. I was rotten inside and he's suffered enough outside. I don't envy him anymore. I'll come to his party, too. Let me pay for it. My thanks for you both has drowned my envy.

Remember where Paul says, "Rejoice with those who rejoice. Weep with those who weep." Who does that? We pretend to do it, but actually the way it usually works is we rejoice with those who weep, and we weep with those who rejoice. The neighbors pour in when you have a hard time because that's easier for them to take. They won't come pouring in as easily upon your good news. Joseph's new coat of many colors drove his brothers to sell him up the river. How delighted would you be if your ten-year-old twin brother got a football uniform for Christmas and you got a pair of socks. That's the way life is. And that's the way we are. As long as we live we don't enjoy some rascal's deathbed repentance any more than the elder brother enjoyed his younger brother coming back to more inheritance.

Weeping with the sad and rejoicing with the happy is a triumph of love. Only love is bighearted enough for such an un-Cainlike act: ". . . Charity envieth not" (1 Corinthians: 13:4). Who do you know who has failed in life, or who has seemed an "also ran," who gets excited by the successes of his friends and loved ones? This may be a far more impressive victory than one's own election to some high honor.

Do you remember the story behind the well-known drawing of the folded hands by the famous artist Albrecht Dürer? Dürer's artist roommate never became famous. God did not seem to smile upon his offering of art any more than He appeared to smile on Cain's. But Dürer's friend took it well. He went to work at hard labor so Dürer could develop his superior talent, until Dürer's friend could no longer paint with his hands. One day Dürer drew the gnarled and work-worn hands of his friend as they were folded in prayer.

Those folded hands went down in history. They have gone around the world. They reach to God and into our hearts better than the hands that grab from envy. For those hands are folded in thanks for someone else who made it and for the blessed opportunity of serving God through him. If you want to know something about handling jealousy and envy, look at those hands.

The first Psalm begins: "Blessed is the man," and Martin Buber translates that word *blessed* as "Oh how happy." Oh how happy is the man whose heart is full of thankfulness to God, and to others, as those folded hands depict so eloquently.

This makes us think of a person who instead of bolting his fast food, squeezes the last drop of sweetness out of his orange. Even raindrops falling on our heads are not to be wasted. "Our daily bread," He said. "In all things be thankful"—a hot shower, a new dress. Wouldn't it be something to have a new car we didn't have to apologize for, or feel guilty about, but felt thankful for.

I still remember walking home from school late one hot September afternoon. It was almost a mile. I think I was in the second grade. Dizzy Dean was pitching in the World Series. By the time I reached our long drive I was so hot and dry and tired I knew I'd never make it to the house. They would find me still lying there by the mailbox in the morning. I threw my books down and lay down in the shade of the old grape arbor and looked up.

I couldn't believe it. I smelled grapes. The grapes were ripe and hanging down in bulging blue clusters. Instantly I was on my feet and it was paradise. God gave the three kings their very own star. And as long as I live I shall remember the luxurious oasis I fell into one day when I was seven and thought I was going to die. The Lord did His first miracle with grapes, for me, too.

Thanks is not simply for things. Even for Snoopy,

suppertime is more than just supper. The grapes gave me more than grapes. Christmas goes beyond department stores and stuffed stockings. Who stuffed them? Where did the idea of stuffing them come from? Every single thing we ever get has to be handed to us personally.

Elijah in the desert was not impressed by the ravens that fed him flesh, or simply by the pitcher that wouldn't run dry, but by their connection to God. Elijah could have been bombed by a barn full of groceries and called it luck, or hard work, or snarled, "It's about time," or even passed it off with, "It's nothing compared to all I deserve." Instead it brought Elijah out of his cave and into the light of the lap he was sitting on.

Not even a crucifixion can stop true thanksgiving: "In the Cross of Christ I glory." In fact, all the titans of thanksgiving have usually been born and bred not from bounty but have come scarred and bleeding from some briar patch. It was blind, deaf, and speechless Helen Keller who, out of the agony of her world of silence and darkness, spelled into our hands these words forever: "I thank God for my handicaps for it has been through them that I found myself, my life, and my God."

It was not until Job lost his money, his family, and finally his health, that he found the resources to say such a thank you to God that scholars are still incredulous: "I have heard of thee by the hearing of the ear: but now mine eye seeth thee."

As strange as it seems, appreciation very often pours not from the man who has everything but from the man who has lost everything. I do not understand it, but I know that the convincing shouts of praise to God have spilled from the broken heart, when someone standing bereft in the graveyard has seen clearly for the first time.

Alexandr Solzhenitsyn sweated out the first years of his stretch in prison absorbed by the injustice of being sentenced to such hard labor for so petty a crime as slighting Stalin in a private letter. Then one day he saw into the black depths of his own heart. This time he saw the vanity and murder that he had only noticed in others before. From that moment he began being thankful for his prison term and found himself saying "dear prison" in his prayers.

The huge blessing life has for us is to not be drowned by our difficulties. All the good things surrounding us can obscure the sunrise; for what we truly have is what we have left after we've been robbed. Heaven's true inventory cannot be thoroughly taken until earth is taken away.

Could your broken dream be your blessing in disguise? "All things," Paul said, "work together for good to them that love God"; how else would we ever love God unless all things worked that good in us? All things? Your thing.

Some may remember the movie *Brian's Song*, which told the story of Brian Picolo. Picolo played football fantastically for the Chicago Bears. Then, during one game, he had trouble getting his breath. He guessed the pollen count was high. But it was cancer that took him at twenty-six. Thanksgiving? Yet Gayle Sayres, Brian's teammate, noticed Pic playing a finer game against that tougher foe than he had ever played upon the field. Mysteriously life went deeper, and for far more gains than all the yards that he had made before.

We only know that we must never surrender to bitterness, but fight on as best we can, as the knight who fought with his scabbard after his sword was gone. If it seems to us in our hard time that our life is lost and God is gone, we must look closely. Perhaps only our props have been removed so we may distinguish Him "from whom all blessings flow." In our crises He will not refuse to confer on us a far more remarkable favor than we knew to request. Easter itself was the fruit of a tomb. Thanks be to God. We'll never get there by gritting our teeth, but by rubbing our hands together over what we've already been given.

11

Slipping Through the Needle's Eye

*T*he glory road is jammed at first with religious types who sing out jauntily to fellow travelers, "Well, we're all going to the same place." But one of the hazards for religious people is that they have a tendency to put on weight around the temples. Pride makes the worst fork in the road.

Anyone with bulging pockets and a swelled head has a tough time with the tight squeeze up ahead. The ascent of the Golden String is not on easy street, particularly for religious freight carriers. Jesus warned, "It is easier for a camel to go through the eye of a needle than for a rich man to enter the kingdom of God" (Matthew 19:24 RSV).

Whether Jesus meant by "the eye of a needle," the low gate in Jerusalem's wall that required camels to kneel to enter, or whether "the eye of a needle" was another of Jesus' oriental exaggerations, such as his comment about those who ". . . strain out a gnat, and swallow a camel" (Matthew 23:24), both interpretations show that no traveler well-heeled enough for three meals a day, can smuggle his pedestal or his property through these customs. Anyone who expects to make it all the way must travel light, "because strait is the gate, and narrow is the way, which leadeth unto life . . ." (Matthew 7:14).

Pride is the dragon mother that feeds predominantly on the religious. A profession of faith is a dangerous thing. In some ways it is safer to be a sinning nobody. God Himself prefers the curses of the profane to the prayers of the pious braggart. Even thanks can be seduced by pride as in Jesus' parable where the Pharisee prayed, ". . . God, I thank thee that I am not like other men, extortioners, unjust, adulterers, or even like this tax collector" (Luke 18:11, 12 RSV).

That prayer was no thanks really, for that Pharisee was taking credit instead of giving thanks. This is the trouble that dogs the people mothers are so proud of. They think they're it. And that's what most of hell is made of—not just bad people but people who think they're it.

It was pride that mothered the devil. He seemed quite nice really: likeable, well dressed, and legal, except for the first commandment, and breaking that one is so common he gets away with it. The devil is an angel who wanted God's seat. That is what twisted him and felled Adam. But

God is a jealous God: "Thou shalt have no other." Nothing upsets God more than competition.

Nothing threatens the religious front-runner as much as pride, and pride does it as subtly as the snake in the garden. If one notices Jesus' devastating attacks on the Pharisees, one grasps how their rivalry threatened Him far more than Rome or the criminal world.

Consider the plight of the returning prodigal. His problems were bad enough in the far country, but he no sooner shaped up and returned home than he was tempted to feel "one up" on all those other prodigals still out there carrying on the same life he had just left. Any former prodigal is soon patting himself on the back for his reform, perhaps even putting his reform in God's place. Pride is such a smooth operator it can avoid violence and scandal, sitting ever so properly in the best seats in the House of God. How easily I can persuade myself that I am heaven-bound, and then with scarcely detectable condescension I'll imply

> You can be, too, if you listen to me carefully. I'll even be good enough to get up in the pulpit and tell you how. Better yet, read this. I'll be kind enough to let you in on this for an offering—not as far in as I am of course, for I've been at this longer.

Pride devours first those who think they've mastered it best.

Christ's Gospel is rigged for comedy. Like the Pharisee praying, we, too, populate hell with extortioners, adulterers, and all those bad guys who wouldn't come to church nor give a nickel for our little sermons to them. But according to Christ, hell suggests religious folks who've choked on famous last words like: "I used to be proud."

A Sunday school teacher taught her class about Jesus' parable of the Pharisee praying: "I thank God I am not like other men." Then she told her class, "Now let us thank God we're not like that Pharisee." If we don't watch out we'll find ourselves thinking, if not saying, *Thank God we're not like that Sunday school teacher;* and on and on goes this inescapable snare that is all the worse for carrying with it some kind of anesthetic that smiles it off.

One church gave their minister a medal for humility, but the next Sunday they took it away, for he wore it. Gert Behanna, that colorfully redeemed prodigal, kept rediscovering her own tragic-comic struggle with pride: "I'm a snob. I look down on people who look down on people."

The villain in the New Testament may not be Judas but the prodigal's elder brother. Judas, in fact, betrayed Christ to those elder brothers who sent Christ to Pilate demanding and staging the Crucifixion. Pilate actually tried to talk them out of it. Rome complied with Christ's execution because of the pressure from these religious experts such as Paul said he had been. And, except for several brief comments about Judas, the opposing forces, which Jesus resoundingly condemned repeatedly throughout His ministry, were Israel's professional leaders.

The prodigal is in the wrong in Jesus' story, but he repents. But the elder brother is frozen in the proud faith of his fathers. He can think of nothing to apologize for, or be thankful for, the only two ways pride can be broken. The elder brother insists, "I never disobeyed you," and "You never gave me a kid to feast with my friends." So what does he need God for? God never did anything for him. He doesn't need God to do anything for him, for he's a self-made man and he never did anything wrong. He was too good to be true to God; going into the banquet hall was beneath him.

The elder brother refers to his baby brother as "this son of yours." His baby brother was not someone he loved or forgave. He treated him like a headache; *good riddance,* he thought. That's what pride did to the elder brother. It was the elder brother who tattled on the prodigal, ". . . who has devoured your living with harlots . . ." (Luke 15:30 RSV). How did the elder brother know that? The proud suspect the worst in others, but give themselves the benefit of the doubt. The proud insinuate: "When I get to heaven, you'll get what's coming to you."

According to the most famous of all the church fathers, Augustine, there are three headshrinking requirements to be Christian. Pride will make us dismiss them when we hear them and prevent us from taking them seriously. They are, first, humility, second, humility, and, third, humility. No one can make it through heaven's gate built in Jerusalem's wall without getting down low enough that his ego can pierce this needle's eye.

Is anything harder to take than working one's head off to be a good person, then watching some thief get away with murder at the last minute by a deathbed repentance? Leading the life of Riley is bad enough but what is worse is religious people who resent those who do lead the life of Riley and get away with it by reversing course in the nick of time.

Here you and I are, Sunday after Sunday, earning brownie points listening to interminable sermons, while these absentees, who never cracked a Bible in their whole lives, sneak under the wire on a splash of grace. It's as though we have to pay the prodigal's fare as well as our own. Pride makes us complainers: "It isn't fair."

This is where we're wrong, where our pride has us by the throat. If we *are* any good, if we *are* innocent, it is not through anything *we* have done. "No one is good except God." It is simply not possible for anyone to deserve credit. If we got what we deserved, we'd be dead. Any boasting, implied or explicit, is a sign that we've become pride's victims: "For by grace you have been saved through faith; and this is not your own doing, it is the gift of God—not because of works, lest any man should boast" (Ephesians 2:8, 9 RSV).

So Jesus advised, "When you are invited, go and sit in the lowest place . . ." (Luke 14:10 RSV). Obviously those suffering from inferiority complexes must first find whatever recognition it takes to satisfy that adolescent deprivation. For we must have some pride in order to finally sacrifice it, but even the most conscientious mother must finally get over the mad desire for her child to be president. She must learn to pray that the child will one day know the joy that can come only through anonymity. ". . . let not thy left hand know what thy right hand doeth . . . and thy Father which seeth in secret himself shall reward thee openly" (Matthew 6:3, 4).

What are we after really? Not the top of the ladder. This compulsion to become a movie star or a VIP has got to stop. Jesus did not say, "Strive to become a celebrity." He suggested, "Take a back seat." Even on the witness stand in the revival tent our aim must not be to steal the show from other less eloquent witnesses. "When thou prayest, enter into thy closet, and when thou hast shut thy door, pray . . ." (Matthew 6:6). We pray for relief from this everlasting restlessness to be "up there with the best of them." Our fun is to come instead from enjoying others' triumphs, from luxuriating in what we have, in getting excited over singing God's praises, not in this competitive religious rat race.

Ideally the saints prayed to do good deeds in the shadows but have a poor memory about them, so that they would not be caught doing it for thanks, or for show. The saints were not after recognition from the public. Their delight was to do God's will. Their meat and drink was pleasing God. Columba on Iona prayed, "Allow that I may keep a door in Paradise; that I may keep the smallest door, the furthest door, the darkest, coldest door that is least used, the stiffest door, if so it be but in thine house, O God."

What would make us happy? Grabbing the seats to Christ's right and His left won't do it, neither will a palace. James Thurber wrote: "The world is so full of a number of things I am sure we should all be happy as kings. And you know how happy kings are." No. Wipe it right out of your mind. We've been misinformed, for the word is: "Blessed are the meek: for they shall inherit the earth" (Matthew 5:5).

To stay on this road we're on, to make it through its keyhole, we must abandon all thought of trying to get ahead. Getting ahead of whom? What does it matter if they pass me by? To get to heaven's gate built in Jerusalem's wall means leaving it in God's hands. We take the lowest seat we can find, leaving it to Him to say, "Friend, come up higher." It is the meek, the ones not watching out for themselves, not doing this for the reward but for the joy of doing it, who will "inherit the earth." Passing out seats is God's part; our part is to serve, not to gloat over others.

In *One Day in the Life of Ivan Denisovich,* fellow inmates noticed the prisoner praying. They ridiculed him: "Prayers won't help you get out of prison any faster." He replied, "I don't pray to get out of prison but to do the will of God." The needle's eye has to do not with our doing something because of what's in it for us but because He wants us to do it. "I am the way, the truth and the life." We take the route of the Golden String for God's sake and for others' sake; not for what we want to get, but for what God wants to give us.

The lowest seat is to be on our face at God's feet with something of the attitude of Betty Scott Stamm who gave her life for Christ in China. That's the way we'll thread the needle with gold. She prayed:

> *Lord, I give up my own plans*
> > *and purposes*
> *All my own desires*
> > *and hopes*
> *And accept Thy will for my life.*
> *I give myself, my life, my all,*
> *Utterly to Thee*
> *To be Thine forever.*
> *Fill me and seal me with Thy Holy Spirit.*
> *Use me as Thou wilt.*
> *Work out Thy whole will in my life*
> *At any cost now and forever.*

12

Fighting Off the Death Wish

Chief Dan George, in the film *Little Big Man*, liked to say, "This is a good day to die," and finally he picked out one of those good days. He dressed in his splendid burial robes, did a little death dance, then with his arms spread-eagle he thanked the Great Spirit for "bringing me to the path that leads nowhere." He climbed up on his death roost, closed his eyes, folded his hands, and decided to die.

But it began to rain. As it poured down he asked, "Am I still in this world?" And his grandson said, "Yes,

Grandfather." The chief replied, "I was afraid of that." Then he got up from his deathbed and went down to supper sighing, "Sometimes the magic works, and sometimes it doesn't."

The will to live should one day turn into the will to die. There's nothing wrong with Great-grandmother's announcement that she will go home after her 102nd birthday in the fall. Clinging to life on earth at any price can also become pathological. There are some things we should rather die than do, just as an old Scotsman would not overpay for a kidney. The will to live, when it is healthy, is eager to leave earth for life over there, as Robert Louis Stevenson said it: "Gladly would I live and gladly die."

Death is not just one more failure down at the hospital. For some it may be high time—it may be overdue. How many kidneys do you deserve? How many heart and lung machines should you tie up for how long? Some patients wearied with several transplants are embarrassed that they may have missed the bus. There are fates far worse than death, and the time comes when we need to join the chorus with Chief Dan George—"This is a good day to die."

However, with that caution, the will to live is of unbelievable importance. You cannot live well and long without it. Great-grandmother is not the only one who calls the shots; you and I also die when we want to. There are far more options than suicide's epidemic of razor blade, rope, and sleeping pills. The death angel comes at your invitation in subtler, even subconscious ways. This, too, is a fork in the road that we must face.

In the Gulag Archipelago, convicts who had given up

hope and were already dead on their feet, were called "goners." They might shuffle along listlessly in line and stare vacantly a few more weeks, but they were like snakes whose heads had been cut off; it takes a while for the news of the coup de grace to trickle to the rest of the body.

So we are not simply at the mercy of stray microbes or arbitrary viruses and deficient organs. We sentence ourselves. We give the signal to give up. Dr. Paul Tournier said in his *Medicine of the Person*, "Men don't die, they kill themselves." And Dr. Walter Menninger, of the famed Menninger Clinic, agreed: "In the end each one kills himself in his own selected way, fast or slow, soon or late."

The June 28, 1986, issue of *Woman's Day* magazine tells of two women who had the same complaint. Their X rays and surgery were almost identical. One died within the year and the other is alive and well. Dr. Walter E. O'Donnell believed that the difference between their life and death was the will to live. Fire at will. Die at will.

Suicide is alarming among children now, to say nothing of teenagers. Eleven-year-old Robbie, whose backyard joined ours, moped around destructively with a woebegone face; his father had deserted Robbie for his job. His mother simply disliked him; and neighbors like me ignored him. One night he sobbed to the baby-sitter: "Nobody loves me. I don't have any friends." He used to lie down on the railroad tracks. They finally found him hanging in an abandoned warehouse.

The causes aren't very complicated. Take away friends, father, and mother, and it takes the heart out of living. Who wants to live without love? Or too much father or mother and too little freedom to be oneself or be alone can suffocate one like a wet blanket. Our will to live folds under too much pressure just as it does in a vacuum.

Senility can creep up on adults for these same reasons, and from the uselessness that attends this deprivation. Arteries harden from obsolescence just as from cholesterol. One's brain becomes about as useful to him as his tonsils. Can't remember what it's for? Let it go, it's no longer needed. It wasn't worn out. It had not been malfunctioning. It was simply unwanted.

In *The Will to Live* by Arnold A. Hutschnecker, M.D., a physician speaks of a woman suffering from an advanced tuberculosis of the lung. She insisted on delaying surgery. Suddenly, she got better. "The final objective proof came when the sputum repeatedly failed to show tubercular bacilli." Then one evening her physician saw her walking. She recognized his car, and waved. "Exuberant joy radiated from her face, a face amazingly transformed. Her hollow cheeks had filled out and a fine tan had smoothed away the lines of bitter resignation. She confessed that she was ecstatically happy. It seemed that our patient had fallen in love again."

Her physician concluded: "I could not have found a mightier ally in our battle against illness. . . . A medical chart records any illness a patient has had in his life. Everything from whooping cough to German measles is duly registered there. But events of striking force such as the birth or death of a love, the beginning or end of a life work . . . are the events which turn and twist a life. These are the verdicts of life and death."

Jesus deals specifically with the will to live in the fifth chapter of Saint John:

Now there is in Jerusalem near the Sheepgate a pool called in Hebrew Bethzatha, which has five colonnades. In these there used to lie a great number of people who were sick, blind, lame, or paralyzed. There was one man there who had been sick for thirty-eight years. Jesus saw him lying there, and finding that he had been in this condition for a long time, said to him, "Do you want to get well?"

The sick man answered, "I have nobody, sir, to put me into the pool when the water stirs, but while I am getting down someone else steps in ahead of me." Jesus said to him, "Get up, pick up your mat, and walk!" And the man was immediately cured, and he picked up his mat and walked. . . . Afterward, Jesus found him in the Temple, and said to him, "See! You are well again. Give up sin, or something worse may happen to you."

John 5:2–9, 14 GOODSPEED

Was the man hanging around the temple as "a ne'er-do-well"? When Jesus said *sin* in this instance, did He mean the sin against life? Jesus went where folks were falling apart. Apparently a few had fallen into that pool and felt better, so others as good as dead dragged themselves there for a desperate, halfhearted effort.

This man had been lying around there for over a generation, at least lying around.

Jesus' question related to the man's will to live: *Do you want to get well?* If you crawl to the doctor's office, he assumes you want to get well, but Jesus had to go after this patient. True, the man was in the pool's vicinity, but he had been locked so long in that position, no wonder Jesus asked him if he wanted to be healed. The patient didn't bring it up. Jesus did. And the sick man didn't jump at the chance. He did not say, "I'd give anything to be well. Name your price, physician." No, he's in no hurry to get up. Instead of saying yes he stalls with excuses.

Jesus of course healed him despite his lukewarm response, but later warned him when He saw him wandering in the temple, that he'd be worse off if he didn't embrace life. Jesus must have meant something like this, suggesting that His patient was wasting time in the temple itself.

We turn Christ into a policeman, but He was the Lord of Life. We turn the Book of Life into the rule book. Of course, breaking rules is breaking life, but Jesus was not nosing out infractions. He was a transmitter of life. One leper cried to Him, "If you wanted, you could make me clean." "Want to? Of course I want to," said Jesus, "That's what I do, my work; I am the life—be clean." We give the impression that if Christ's around, you better be good, or you'll catch it, like saying, "Don't swear; here comes the preacher." To the contrary, when Christ comes around, you better look alive. Christ's chief enemy is death.

Some of Buddha's contributions coincide with Christ's, but Buddha was not only unenthusiastic about finding himself on earth, he recommended suicide philosophically. Buddha distrusted all desire and suggested the eightfold path by which to eradicate it. But the psalmist panted for God like an antelope for water.

Buddha was big on denial, weak on hallelujahs. We could use Buddha's patience, but his path was one of religious sedation. Buddha would be horrified to hear Christ cry, "Be of good *cheer*, I have overcome the world." For Buddha came that we might have death and have it more abundantly.

But in our Book, even desperate Job refused to "curse

142

God and die," as his wife suggested. Job insisted in the end that life was worth going through hell for. Our God says, "I have set before you life and death. *Choose life.*"

Only three suicides embarrass the Bible, and we are taught to doubt their success. Christ's first miracle was to turn water into the wine of life, and His last was to invite a desperado into the life beyond.

The will to live here also comes from our love of life over there. Moms and dads, or somebody who loves us, not too much, nor too little, a job we love to do—all fuel our will to live forever. For finally, our will to live hinges on our belief in heaven. If you lose hope in immortality, you finally lose heart for mortality too. If you love someone, you'll be incapable of despair over them even upon their death. Hope is irrepressible where there's love.

Mark Twain's mother was nearly an invalid in her early years. Then she overcame it and lived hale and hearty into her nineties. Twain speaks of her tenderly in his autobiography. Twain observed that most people were interested in a few things, but the remarkable difference about his mother was that she was interested in *everything*, including the life to come. It was this, he believed, that maintained her.

I have been reading about C. G. Jung, Freud's most distinguished student—most recently in a book entitled *Not God*, which pays tribute to Jung's contribution to the birth of Alchoholics Anonymous. At the conclusion of Jung's incredibly long practice as a psychotherapist, he declared in his *Modern Man in Search of a Soul*, "All the patients who came to me over thirty-five years of age fell ill because they lost their faith in God or immortality, and none of them were healed until they regained that belief."

It is almost as though Jung quoted Christ: "Rejoice not, that the spirits are subject unto you; but rather *rejoice*, because your names are written in heaven" (Luke 10:20 *italics mine*).

Jung confessed that he could not explain it, but just as the body, for some reason we do not know, needs salt to be healthy, so the soul of man needs to have faith that its fate is secure beyond death.

While our will to live is sabotaged by a bad childhood and a lonely and useless life, our will to live is also a matter of will. For years I blamed my disbelief in God on my education; in a way I was evading belief because I told myself I was too smart for it. But the truth was, I didn't want to believe. My selfish will was in the way. Our mind thinks up ways to justify our wishes.

Muggeridge says there is a death wish in Communists— a hatred of God. They despise love. They turn their backs on life. They are against heaven. They do not want it. They will it not to be. That streak runs through the West, through our journals, our campuses, even our own hearts. All of us struggle with these principalities of sarcasm. We wrestle with our bitterness, our fear, but also, finally, with the deepest longing in our hearts. What *will* it be? "I have set before you life and death. Choose life!"

I asked a sophisticated lady in Boston to explain her belief that she had been healed of a malignancy. She said she told God that if He wished her to die she was as ready as she would ever be and would go peacefully, but if agreeable to Him she preferred to live. She believed that she was healed through that conversation. Ultimately, we need God to help us determine whether to live here or there. Perhaps the will to live depends on our will to do the will of God.

This chapter on the will to live ends the way the Book of Psalms begins:

Blessed is the man that walketh not in the counsel of the ungodly, nor standeth in the way of sinners, nor sitteth in the seat of the scornful . . . and he shall be like a tree planted by the rivers of water, that bringeth forth his fruit in his season; his leaf also shall not wither; and whatsoever he doeth shall prosper.

Psalms 1:1, 3

PART III

ALL
THE
WAY
HOME

13

The Path Through Despair You Have Provided Me

*B*eginning with the Bible as our starting block, we can face the forks in the road until we finally come almost in sight of the spires of the city of God. But for some, the hard part of the journey may be near home, as it was for Christ in Gethsemane; the Golden String shines its brightest there.

For many, life begins with a Cross and continues uphill all the way home; but even the sunniest life sooner or later falls into the valley of the shadow of death, perhaps when someone who means everything is taken from us. The

149

road dead ends and the lights go out. All our neat professions of faith and high hopes and dreams are dashed to pieces as though we were no better off than the most bitter unbeliever. Here we were, safely winding the sacred cord into a ball when suddenly, as the old ballad moaned, "The golden cord is severed and our hopes in ruin lie."

That is why simply following Jesus is not enough. As we approach this vicious washout in the road we require the overwhelming comfort and consolation accomplished by His Cross. Life finally dishes out more than anyone can take. Sooner or later we're shot down. We're wiped out. Without the incredible assist of the Cross of Christ we're done for. His Cross is crucial to our making it across life's impossible intersection of good and evil. Somehow the Cross connects these split ends of the Golden String.

A friend of ours is terribly scarred from head to foot as the result of a battle in World War II. It occurs to one seeing him in swimming trunks that he must have returned from the dead. On one occasion he spoke of how it happened. It was during the Battle of the Belgian Bulge, the Germans' last desperate attempt to escape defeat. His platoon was retreating in single file, each one stepping carefully in the steps of the one ahead to minimize the danger in going through mined territory. He was last in line. In the darkness he was separated from his unit and stepped on a mine.

When he regained consciousness he found himself alone. He was able to see that a river was ahead of him, and that his company had safely crossed it. He lay in evacuated, if not enemy, territory. He had to somehow get over there too. He could not move his legs, so using his arms he dragged himself to the river. He could go no farther and passed out.

When he came to, he was on the other side of the river. He did not know how. And to this day no one has told him how he got across. That illustrates how God's heaven touches hell in all our lives. There is a crossing we all must make that is completely impenetrable to human efforts, though human hands are often used. The impact of Christ's Cross somehow triggers a deep connection in our souls that breaches this insurmountable obstacle.

It happened that time at the Red Sea, and it happens for each of us, at our own last great river to cross. This is why we sing "In the Cross of Christ I Glory," why there is no better talisman for us to carry on this journey, and why in danger we should reach for the Cross more quickly than the highwayman would draw his gun.

The Cross of Christ is the old, old story of how someone took despair in the blackest hour and turned it into a path for you and me. Just as the three kings could travel only at night when the star could be seen, one lonely Friday afternoon when the sky went so black a man could not see his fist in front of his face, the center Cross exploded the wall of death, and such light poured from the opening He made that it fulfilled the psalmist's boast: "The darkness shines as in the daytime." It is as each of us adore this Cross that there opens "The path through despair you have provided me."

Mention the Cross nowadays and immediately people think of a prominent Texas silversmith, thus setting off a discussion about exquisite designs to choose from and with such a wide price range.

However, at the time of Christ, when Imperial Rome

ruled the world, the mention of the word *cross* chilled one to the bone. The English are known for rope to hang people; the French for a guillotine to chop off their heads; we Americans keep law and order with an electric chair. But all this is kid stuff.

The Romans were past masters at the terror of torture and over the centuries perfected their expertise until they came up with the last turn of the screw, the cross. Strange that we should still be wearing that wretched thing.

A crucifixion was much more than a heavy post planted in the ground with a huge crossbeam that the condemned criminal had carried there. (When I visited Golgotha I was shown ancient holes drilled in deeply embedded stone into which successive crosses were supposedly inserted.) A crucifixion was a municipal sporting event.

Once the victim had been tried and sentenced, he was turned over to the Roman soldiers to play with in a mock trial. Deep markings still evident on the original paving stones in Jerusalem bear grim testimony to that game of kings the Roman soldiers exacted of the victim, gambling, too, for whatever he had on him.

An agonized death was not enough for the greedy spectators. The guard dressed up their doll in purple, crowned him with excruciating thorns, subjecting him to their version of God save the king. Then they practically beat the man to death, dropped the crossbeam on his battered back and dogged him to the contraption where he would hang till he suffocated. While hanging on a cross, one has to raise himself up for each breath until he can't do it anymore. It might take a couple of days.

Very religious people forced Rome to crucify Christ. We still cannot get it through our heads. Imagine your respected teachers and preachers, everybody who was anybody, pulling such an awful stunt. It wasn't criminals, nor Communists, nor the Mafia, it was bishops and senators, among the most highly spiritual people you'll ever know, when the crime rate was low; don't we love the Old Testament? Well, this was done by the very people who gave it to us.

It wasn't a close decision either. Except for Nicodemus, Gamaliel, and Pilate dragging his feet, it was unanimous. The Gospels say that "all the disciples forsook Him and fled." The treasurer of Christ's inner circle sold Him to the police to make ends meet. Christ's second-in-command rejected Him publicly three crucial times.

I like to think I would have done differently, but you and I are only human like those people. Each year in Lent we reenact this ancient drama in hope that we shall finally see through its theatre to our own part in this evil madness that desires to rid our world of God. The evil we project on the Near East or beyond the Iron Curtain pierces our own heart like a dagger: "Were you there when they crucified my Lord? Sometimes it causes me to tremble." People say they became Christian as though at a Sunday school picnic. No, it happens when one is jolted by the sight of His blood on our hands.

In a way the mob on Golgotha that killed Christ was blessed, at least by finally becoming aware of what they had done. It broke them. They became so appalled that they stampeded from the hill, beating their breasts. His last words shook them off the place of the skull. It put the sun out for three hours. No one there would ever be the same again. They were suffering not only from fear but also from awe at the power and the glory of His forgiveness.

Whatever the Cross is, it is somehow our logo. It is something we helped make. Whatever we are, we are Crossmakers. They say we are firebuilders, carnivores, toolmakers, but that's a superficial reading. We're killers, not only like Cain, but like that mob—God killers; we'll read out others' goodness every time, so we won't look so bad. Otherwise, we would not need redemption, just a little help would do.

So Christ took this very Cross that we built—the same nails we hammered into the hand that fed us—and turned our instrument of torture into the tool to save us. Those of us who are only human characteristically build a good solid cross and, in our own way, hang God on it. In some way or another we can even pervert our pursuit of the Golden String to save our own skin, until we think we have Christianity rigged to suit ourselves; but that's where we're wrong. He has us there. From that snug bunker we've misbuilt with our belief He'll break your heart, finally, for good.

We like to say God created the world, stars, day, and night. And He truly did do a lot back then, mountains and all. But it's nothing compared to His performance on the Cross. You haven't seen anything until you've seen Him die for you.

We needed birth to be, but we can never be truly born without the surgery of the Cross. When a child asks, "Who is God?" we usually answer, "The One who made everything," but we must hasten to add, "the One who is remaking everything from the Cross." Tell your child not only what God did in the beginning but also what He did when He was treed like an animal. Obviously the first week of days or aeons was important enough to begin our

Bible. But the crucial week that put the Bible together was Holy Week. That Good Friday broke the back of earth's erosion and began the comeback that we approach as we wind the string in our hands.

The lost little girl was right. She was no more than three, sobbing as if her heart would break at the police station. She was too small and distraught to tell them her last name or her address. Between sobs she managed at last to say, "Take me to the hill where the white cross stands. I can find my way home from there."

You and I, too. In the maze of very scholarly interpretations and nice distinctions, and all the dust raised by saints and sinners struggling in lost and found, the only way we can get high and low, left and right, church and unchurched together—without driving each other off the road to glory—is for us to go back to the hill where the white Cross stands. Only then can we find our way home.

I do not qualify as a Pentecostal, but I have many friends who are and I have learned much from them, including this enlightenment from the distinguished Pentecostal, Dr. Derek Prince, as he preached from Romans 8:9: "Now if any man have not the Spirit of Christ, he is none of his."

> There are many people who've been baptized in the Holy Spirit, who speak in tongues, who work miracles, but who demonstrate little or nothing of the Spirit of Christ. And the mark that makes us God's is not speaking in tongues, nor is it working miracles, nor is it preaching tremendous sermons. It's having the Spirit of Christ.

And there is no way we can better explain the Spirit of Christ than to point to the Cross. That's how we know about "a broken and contrite spirit." "Did e'er such love and sorrow meet, or thorns compose so rich a crown?" Think of the Spirit of Him who carried that heavy Cross and "never said a mumblin' word," whose last tears fell for the city that crushed Him, and whose dying words went out to a thief in welcome. It was that Cross that shattered the evil in the centurion standing guard. It was the first shadow of that Cross that fell on that rich old ruler Nicodemus early in Passion Week and swept him into the kingdom to help Joseph get Him down from there before that week was out.

Do you know for whom the center Cross was made? Barabbas, if not you and me. Jesus took our place. The center Cross is ours. He took it. He died for us.

When we come at last to this seeming dead end we can find our way home. We sing "Amazing Grace . . . that saved a wretch like me." We must not take the word *wretch* out of it. Having the Spirit of Jesus means we know we deserved to die instead of Him. We're no better than anyone else. Only as a wretch can we keep from condescending to another wretch.

What do I glory in? That I've been found? That I am better off? Better able? No. "In the Cross of Christ I glory."

And the consequence of glorying in the Cross is a sharp right turn; at this fork in the road we "pour contempt on all our pride," thus losing our contempt for others and finding compassion for them.

You may remember the powerful movie and play *A Raisin in the Sun* by Lorraine Hansberry. It tells the story of a poor black family from Chicago's Southside. After the father's death, the mother wants to use his insurance money to move her family into a little house on the other side of town.

Her son wants to use the money to go into business. He has never had a break and never had a job. Now he has a friend who has a "deal." He begs for the money, and although his mother refuses to give it to him at first, she eventually knows that she must give in. How can she deny her son's pleading for his first chance to do something for the family?

Soon the family learns that the son's "friend" has taken the money and skipped town. Humiliated, the son confesses it's true. His sister wastes no time tearing into him. Pouring out her contempt, she screams at him for having lost, for them all, the only route out of the hell in which they have lived for years.

When the sister finishes her tirade, her mother speaks,

> "I thought I taught you to love him."
> "Love him? There is nothing left to love."
> "There is always something left to love. And if you ain't learned that, you ain't learned nothing. Have you cried for that boy today? I don't mean for yourself and for the family 'cause we lost the money. I mean for him; what he been through and what it done to him. Child, when do you think is the time to love somebody the most; when they done good and made things easy for everybody? Well then, you ain't through learning—because that ain't the time at all. It's when he's at his lowest and can't believe in hisself 'cause the world done whipped him so. When you starts measuring somebody, measure him right, child, measure him right. Make sure you done taken into account what hills and valleys he come through before he got to wherever he is."

I don't know who first made the sign of the Cross. Who do you suppose emerged from that horror of His mangled death and decided it was meant to be, that it had to be. And finally, instead of running from the Cross as the disciples did that Friday, someone started making the sign of the Cross. Who do you suppose had the nerve to do it first?

Was it old Nicodemus, after helping Joseph get Him down? Do you suppose that night he saw crosses everywhere he stared even in his sleep, finally doodling one on the ground? Did Mary Magdalene drag her finger in the sand and find herself making one? Surely the Cross was branded on Mother Mary's mind. Did she out of desolation paint a cross of ashes on her head? Perhaps Peter was alone, slumped in the bottom of his boat whittling a piece of wood that turned into a Cross. And when he realized what he had done, something let loose in him and he began weeping, not bitterly this time, but letting in a flood of light.

All I know is that you find crosses everywhere now. And I see fingers clinging to them as they leave this place.

My young friend Jeff was heavily into drugs. His suffering became extreme and at last he lay inert in a hospital bed from an overdose of angel dust from which they were unable to rouse him. But something happened during his last hours that no one could explain. And no one would want to miss. There was a crucifix bolted to the wall of his room. No one knows how he did it, but somehow during that coma Jeff got out of bed and wrenched it off the wall and clung to it and wouldn't let anyone take it from him.

There are those of us here today who haven't yet believed. And perhaps are held back till someone shows compassion on them as Celia did for battered and con-

fused Sophie in that remarkable film *The Color Purple.*
Looking back on that kindness she received in her dark
hour, Sophie said, "It was then I knew that there was a
God." Someone will help you tear that Cross from off the
wall and you, too, will see your way clearly before you.
"For when I think that God His Son not sparing sent Him
to die, I scarce can take it in."

"Jesus keep me near the Cross."

14

To Keep
You Company
on the
Way

*H*ell is our being cut off. Ever hear about someone who got lost alone in a wilderness for a few hours? Such an experience can soon reduce one to a jabbering idiot. Prisoners call solitary confinement "the hole." When a mental patient withdraws into isolation he can become a vegetable. Many of us enjoy being alone but there are limits. No one has lived very long if he hasn't had to bite his lip hard at times to keep from crying, "Don't leave me." The secret to the trail is not only good direction, but finding someone to keep us company not only on the way, but all the way home.

And the good old U.S.A., for all its technological marvels and social triumphs, may suffer from loneliness more than any other nation on earth. Record-breaking crowds in sports arenas and television antennas thicker than trees have not covered our feelings of abandonment.

America may still be the land of opportunity, but it is also heartbreak hill, as I discuss at more length in my book *Amazed by Grace*. Americans suffer from heart trouble more than people in any other country on earth. Scandinavia and Japan, for instance, have only a fraction of the incidents of heart difficulties that devastate our country.

The research of Dr. James Lynch of Harvard shows that our heart problems do not result simply from improper diet and lack of exercise but also have to do with our estrangement. Did you know which state in the United States has the highest incidents of heart ailments? Nevada. Las Vegas and Reno are not only known for gambling and divorce, they also have a highly mobile and rather rootless population. The people there don't settle in houses, they camp in hotels. Nevada is still unsettled. It appeals to drifters.

Nevada's neighboring state, Utah, has the lowest rate of heart difficulties in the nation. Dr. Lynch and others feel that this is no accident, but has to do with the highly stable family life of its devoutly religious residents.

Research in hospitals seems to bear out the fact that loneliness can threaten the heart. The heart of one comatose patient studied showed remarkable improvement when the nurse held his hand. Individual hearts seemed able to undergo sustained strain when supported by friendship. One's cardiac health has to do with being in dependable rapport. Bear Bryant, the famed college football coach, wasn't kidding about what gave his winning teams strength and endurance. He explained, "I gave them one heartbeat."

Your heart is an index to how near and dear you are to others. When relationships break down, so do hearts. Heart trouble may have something to do with heartache.

Whether or not subsequent research supports this theory, the Bible teaches us not simply to do right, but to seek right relationships.

I may have been one of the most disappointing milers Western Michigan ever had, but God gave me a gift that enabled me to eat the cinders that flew in my face from those in front. Our other miler ran beside me. I never lost him. I could always hear him breathing during every race we ever ran. He was not out to get me. He was on my side. What a comfort he was to me. He made it possible for me to finish with all I had, no matter how much it hurt. In the third lap when my chest was on fire and I knew I was going to die, because there wasn't enough air in all creation to fill my lungs, that red-headed guy was always there to push me through.

One of the Greek words for the Holy Spirit is *Paraclete*. It derives from those athletic people, from the word for one who runs alongside a fainting soldier and cheers him on. According to Dr. Theodore Williams of India, "He keeps the one who is reaching the breaking point from breaking."

God is not simply the One who created everything in the beginning and who will pick up everything in the end and put it back together. He is, as Abraham and Moses detected, a traveling companion.

Someone will often sigh that the patriarchs and judges of the Old Testament enjoyed conversation with God that we moderns miss, as though God was nearer before Christ than since; but that isn't true. Christ not only made our way clearer by His example and easier by His Cross, He is powerfully with us in Spirit.

God came down to earth as the prophets predicted. His name is Immanuel, God with us, in a way they were previously without. The one God, the Father, to whom Abraham prayed, turned into the three in One for us. He appeared in the flesh and empowers us now: "I will send you the Holy Spirit, the Comforter." We can say, "In the name of the Father, the Son, and the Holy Pacer."

Abraham and Moses certainly were not taken in by our Santa Claus. But his presence among us testifies to our longing. In a way we've fabricated Santa Claus to fulfill what we've failed to appropriate about the Holy Ghost.

I know a young man of five, who was able to write out his list of requests to Santa Claus and, with no help from anyone else, secretly drop it off at an official slot for North Pole correspondence. No one could shake his list from him: "Don't worry. Santa knows. He'll take care of it." There he was Christmas morning, the most mystified boy on earth because Santa hadn't gotten the message. Solicitous parents finally managed to wrestle his secret requests from him then and ultimately covered for Santa's embarrassing delay.

I am not so upset by that boy's misplaced trust as I am struck by how ready we all are to hang up our stockings. We are born stocking hangers. Before we're three we know what chimneys are for. We're made to believe in a celestial visitor. Santa Claus is a burlesque testimonial, catering to our unfinished nature. There's a God-shaped vacuum in each of us. We are not self-starters, not completely independent. The Quakers called themselves friends, not separate entities, but friends. And friends don't make sense friendless. "What a Friend we have in Jesus."

A young medical student friend of ours from Chillicothe, Ohio, recently told us that one night, a few years ago, his family was notified that his brother's jeep had been crushed by a semi. They rushed to the hospital. The physicians in attendance announced the immediate necessity to amputate both legs. The devout Catholic family conferred and requested another medical opinion which confirmed the first one.

The family still could not bear to make that grisly decision. They drew nearer to one another and to God. Then they felt led to take the boy by ambulance to University Hospital in Columbus, hoping against hope that some way might be found there to save his legs.

An orthopedist here, whom our own family would come to know soon after in similar circumstances, reviewed the grim situation. He said he would try. Then he turned to our student friend and his other brother and assigned them the task of returning to the battered jeep and scouring it for every possible piece and splinter of bone they could find. They were to bring whatever they found to him on ice as fast as they could. They flew to the smashed jeep, threw up at the gory sight, then brought back their precious little collection of bits and pieces of their brother's bones.

Dr. Kubiac performed the operation and the legs were saved. The boy went on in athletics. For those who have ears to hear let them hear: "I will not leave you desolate. I will come to you."

This also applies to those who must go through the valley of the shadow of death. Not every operation succeeds. Not every patient lives to tell about it. But the promise is kept to all, both the quick and the dead. Think of this next story as a proof of the text "I will never leave you nor forsake you."

A poverty-stricken youth, "imprisoned" in a tenant farmer's shack on a cotton plantation, dreamed of becoming a doctor. He prayed to God earnestly and finally kneeled down in the orange Georgia clay and vowed that if God would see him through medical school, he would never let God down.

Somehow doors opened, and he made it. He was finally licensed as a physician. One night after a long day a call came to his home from someone critically ill on the other side of the woods. It was two miles away, night had fallen, and it was starting to snow. He was too tired to go, so he undressed, went to bed, and turned out the light. But lying there in the dark he remembered his childhood vow. He threw off the covers, dressed, and set out through the darkness alone.

About a mile into the woods someone jumped out of the thick black and in a rough voice demanded the time. The doctor put down his bag and pulled out his watch. Mysteriously, the man vanished, and the physician went on to see his patient. On his way home at the same place the fellow interrupted him again, this time asking for a match. Suddenly the man was gone again and the physician returned safely.

The next morning the doctor learned that there had

been a murder in the woods the night before and that a suspect had been caught. He went down to the jail to see who it was. He asked the man behind bars if he had stopped him to ask the time of day the night before. "Yes." "Did you also ask me for a match on my way back?" "Yes." "Why didn't you murder me?" "Because, each time I came out there was someone else with you."

There is another most moving story about this in Daniel three. Three young believers in God were exiled to a foreign city where the king's word was not only law, but divine. The king was to be worshiped. These three boys became the king's favorites, but they refused to bow down to him. This finally sent him into such a fury that he ordered them to be burned to death. The three decided they would not bow to the king whether their God saved them or not.

The fire was so hot that those who threw them in perished immediately. Then the king himself looked into the furnace of fire to see what had happened to the three. "Lo," said the king, "I see four men loose, walking in the midst of the fire, and they have no hurt; and the form of the fourth is like the Son of God"(v.25).

Earth itself already seems like a furnace to some, and for others it's in the making, but our eyes are not on earth, or its fires, but upon the One beside us who will never leave us nor forsake us no matter what happens, helping us to do what we can, what we have to do, what we could never do without Him. Remember this. Now and forever, "you never walk alone." You are walking together into joy.

15

One
Step
at a
Time

No one knows how long our journey is. The big thing about our trip is not only our destination—today is the day. We are playing for keeps, winding the string to eternity, but we never know when we'll crash "Heaven's gate in Jerusalem's wall." "Now is the time of salvation." The big idea is today. Jesus reminded us: "Do not be anxious about tomorrow . . ." (Matthew 6:34 RSV). "Give us this day our daily bread." We have the will to live forever, but "let tomorrow be anxious for itself."

The ancient Greeks wore candles on the toes of their shoes to see as far as one step at a time at night. Life's like that. We can see no farther than the next step. Will there be a war, depression? We can't see overnight. Even the weather still fools us. No country or family can rely on the predictions of astrologers or Jeanne Dixon. "We know not what a day may bring forth." Paul Tillich insisted that we can count on happening what could not possibly be predicted. Life goes on breath after breath, but we can't hoard oxygen, as we can't hoard love. We're stuck with one step at a time.

Tolstoy retold the Russian legend of a king who decided that he would have it made if he knew the answers to three questions: The most important person, the most important thing to do, and the best time to do it. These questions only created controversy among the king's counselors, so he visited a holy man deep in a forest. Since the holy man would only speak with common folk, the king dismounted from his horse, flung off his royal cape and left them with his guards, and walked the short distance to the hermit's hut. The thin old holy man was panting from spading his garden and went on digging even after the king had asked him his three questions.

Getting no answer, the king asked if he could help dig. The holy man thanked him, and while the king was working a man ran up to them and fell down clasping his stomach, the blood spurting between his fingers. The king knelt down exposing the wound and staunched the flow of blood with cloths from the hermit. Then they carried the man into the hut where all of them spent the night.

In the morning the wounded man asked the surprised king to forgive him, explaining that his family had suffered an injustice in the king's court, so he had come out to the woods that day to kill the king. Instead the king's bodyguard had practically killed him and the king had nursed him. The king forgave him and promised to rectify the wrong done. Then the man died.

As the king prepared to leave, he asked the hermit his three questions. The old man told him that he already had his answers:

> Yesterday, had you not dug those beds for me, but had gone your way, that man would have attacked you . . . so the most important time was when you were digging the beds; and I was the most important man; and to do me good was your most important business.
>
> Afterwards, when that man ran to us, the most important time was when you were attending to him. For if you had not bound up his wounds he would have died without making peace with you. So he was the most important man, and what you did for him was your most important business.
>
> Remember then: There is only one time that is important—now! It is the most important time because it is the only time when we have any power. The most necessary man is he with whom you are, for no man knows whether he will ever have dealings with anyone else; and the most important thing is to do him good, because for that purpose alone was man sent into this life.

God is dependable but unpredictable. He likes to keep us in suspense. Perhaps one property of persons is that we're tied to immediacy. Only God is beyond "now." That is why we need Him. He gives us only a few cards at a time in this game we play for keeps. In the wilderness the people of Israel had to gather the manna daily. It wouldn't keep. We're forced to rely on God every single day.

Some cannot enter the present for they are imprisoned in the past. Perhaps someone fancied himself a hero in World War II and must fight those old battles over and over again. He seems unable to leave that former glory. Others remain preoccupied with old loves or surgery, or with their baseball days; some people, if they could have their wish, would prefer to be eighteen again. Nothing has replaced that former personal attractiveness, nothing is left but a nostalgia. Life becomes a closed album, or a baseball record, or a medal.

Jesus does not object to the past. Memories are precious, but they are perverted if they prevent now from happening. The slate is clean. This is a new day. Yesterday's scores cannot be used today. There is no accumulation of points. There is no point to living on, if it's simply a rehash of yesterday. People who make life one perpetual retirement party are already dead. We can live only in now.

There is nothing wrong with someone insisting that they had too much religion as a child, or someone else boasting of the salvation they received twenty years before, but to be preoccupied with history can deny today. We have resentments to uproot today from being force-fed religion yesterday. We have fruit to bear today resulting from any former meeting with Christ.

We are tempted to put things off as well as drag things up. But it is death to live outside of now, death to today. God will not be postponed. Jesus spoke of a man who had so much grain he decided, "I will tear down my barns and build bigger ones to store my grain and eat, drink, and be merry." But God said, "Thou fool, this night thy soul shall be required of thee . . ." (Luke 12:20). We say, "Eat, drink, and be merry for tomorrow we die," but we are mistaken. We die today. We must be ready today, as the old hermit said. Now is all the time there is, for all we know.

Men have tried to outwit this hand-to-mouth existence by consulting the stars, or mediums. "Perhaps we'll not die till the day after tomorrow." We're like W. C. Fields rapidly leafing through his Bible, "Looking for loopholes." But the Bible frowns on such curiosity. King Saul consults the witch of Endor to call up Samuel to find out how the battle will go the next day. She gets Samuel and the news, but it is bad news of defeat and death, and Samuel is irritated. The Bible discourages people from trying to peek at the answers in the back of the book.

Jesus urges us to concentrate on today. "Don't be anxious about tomorrow." Its demands are too much to bear. "Sufficient unto today is the evil thereof."

Even Christ was not clairvoyant. Everyone now is discussing the return of Christ. But Scripture insists that even Christ does not know the target date for His return. He kept busy getting men through today. He was not passing out lottery tickets. Jesus called His disciples to come with Him then. Promises have their place, but when the sick came to Him, He never told them, "You should have come yesterday," or, "Come again tomorrow." "Today if you will harden not your hearts, today He will hear you." He apparently didn't keep an appointment book. He took care of things as they came up. He didn't fight Gethsemane till He got there. As a great coach tells his team, "The most important play is this one."

On the Cross itself, Jesus was not obsessed with how

He got into this mess or when it would be over. It was one thing at a time. "I thirst." "Father, forgive them." And when the thief beside Him turned to Him and said, "Remember me when You come into Your kingdom," Jesus did not reply, "Aren't you a little late coming to this?" Nor did Jesus say, "Well, perhaps after some time in purgatory." No, Jesus, the Man of the hour, poured the past and the future into the present and said, "Today you shall be with me in Paradise."

How long can I hang on? When will my house sell? When will I get over this? These things matter, but they're not the main thing. The main thing is to do today's work. "This is the day that the Lord hath made. Rejoice and be glad in it." And don't let any remorse over yesterday or dread about tomorrow rob you of rejoicing in today. This is where we are—on planet earth today.

Alchoholics Anonymous has reminded us so much of the Gospel that has gotten away from us. They emphasize today, because the drunk who intends to quit drinking at the end of the month is kidding. The one who is ready for A.A. is one who says "No more drinks today," day after day. Augustine said: "Oh, God, make me good but not just yet." That really means don't make me good at all. So long as we delay, we invalidate our resolutions.

I've resented along with many others the revivalist shouting at me to "March down the sawdust trail tonight or else." What's he know? I like to be coaxed, and I don't like my religion loaded with so much fire and brimstone. But in a profound way the evangelist who's preaching for conversion tonight is right, along with any other good salesman. The sale has to be made today. Delay is death to a sale.

God knows that the way I decide now is the way I'll decide tomorrow night, or next year at this time. That's the decision that suits me. That's the way I am. The picture you have of me today will be a good likeness—still sitting in the backseat, or still going to "get around to it"—it's a long way around. It's true. What I decide today is where I'll probably be till my dying day. "Today if you will harden not your hearts." Today truly is your only chance.

So the way to the Holy City is by one day at a time. The long-distance runner makes it stride by stride. Don't look back, and don't try to do things ahead of time. Concentrate on the next step.

In early 1965, I had the pleasure of hearing several lectures by Paul Tournier. Although gray-haired, bent from age and illness, and speaking through an interpreter, he held his audience spellbound. He concluded with a personal experience which I offer as an illustration of timeliness.

Doctor Tournier was an orphan boy who had had great difficulty being accepted and accepting himself. The first significant step toward acceptance came because of the interest his Greek professor took in him. The professor was not religious, but he invited lonely young Paul into his home and into his intellectual world. As Tournier put it, "He reinserted me back into humanity."

Their intimacy never ranged beyond the exchange of ideas, but it represented a great stride for both. Many years later, long after Tournier had become a Christian, he searched his mind for some friend who might read and offer suggestions on his first manuscript before it went to the printer, and he thought of his old Greek professor, by then retired. The professor agreed and asked Doctor

Tournier to read the first chapter to him. When he had finished the chapter Tournier looked up for a critical reaction. The old man said merely, "Paul, continue." He read another chapter. "Paul, continue." He read the third chapter. Then the old teacher said, "Paul, we must pray together." They prayed. Afterward, Tournier exclaimed, "But I didn't know you were a Christian." "Yes." "When did you become a Christian?" "Just now."

So don't worry about having the extra help we'll need on the hard places up ahead; don't be anxious even about the hardest day of all. In *The Hiding Place*, Corrie ten Boom's father asks her: "When you are going on a trip, when do I give you your ticket?" She replies: "Just as I board the train." Then her father says: "That's how God does it, Corrie."

16

The Father
Will Run
and Greet
You Too

*H*ow will it all end? What will become of us? Are you kidding? Am I stringing you along with my bright idea of our actually breaking through heaven's gate? When I am finally up against the wall what if it's hell's gate and not Jerusalem's wall at all? Have you seen the Holy Land lately? It doesn't look very promising, and it's packed with painfully explosive memories.

Even as the ball of Golden String grows in our hands, the prospect of hell has swollen in our minds—and it's not only nuclear. Turn on the radio, and some evangelist will shake you over those eternal fires as bad as Billy Sunday's sermons. Our texts have become bumper stickers: "Jesus is coming and boy is He mad." "Jesus is coming; look busy."

Even churches on the hill have fed us the good news in such a way as to fix it in our heads as bad. People have become dead certain that earth's too far gone for heaven; it's really little more than a recruiting center for hell. By the time God's finished ransacking the late great planet earth, there will be nothing left of it but the late great person, me. The journalist and the preacher have unwittingly joined the suspicious pessimist lurking in our hearts to turn our Golden String into a fuse.

Our situation is serious. No one can dismiss lightly the repeated warnings of Scripture about our approaching confrontation with the judgment of God. One day we will be in for a devastating audit. God will turn on all the lights and the truth will be out before Him "from whom no secrets are hid and all desires known." The agony is too real, and our need for mercy too great, for anyone to be blasé.

We can smile over the comedy of acrobatic pulpiteers, preaching as though they were fighting bees, but Christ wipes off our smile by His stern declaration: "So shall it be at the end of the world: the angels shall come forth, and sever the wicked from among the just, and shall cast them into the furnace of fire: there shall be wailing and gnashing of teeth" (Matthew 13:49, 50).

The theme of this book appreciates that "by Adam's fall we sinned all," and we were somehow shipwrecked offshore from Eden. Another way of putting it would be to say that wormy apples were illicitly imported into the

Garden of Eden itself, and ever since it has been definitely downhill. Men are not only condemned to sweat and women suffer the pains of hard labor, it is as though we are stuck on a dying planet.

The church has taught us to anticipate an ending to creation as sudden as its beginning, but also included is a gradual deterioration. We're not getting any younger, and the ground under our feet is not getting any firmer or more fertile. The mud from which we were made is aging along with us. We're losing ground as well as life. Eagles are not the only endangered species, and tiny meteorites are not the only cosmic time bombs. Our descent is noticeable.

For all the excitement of *Star Wars* decor in Disney World, I find when I fantasize where I want to go, that A.D. 2091 does not hold my attention as much as, for instance, Williamsburg. Somehow, where we came from carries a greater significance that leaks away as we go on and on into a more and more nebulous future.

With all the fascination we have for modern technology, which brought all the blessed breakthroughs that have delivered us from typhoid and bloodletting as well as battered hips, I can't tell you how enchanted I was one day in the sun under the blue sky of Williamsburg.

I've seen the introductory film *The Story of a Patriot* three times now, rightly unchanged for the last twenty years. It opens as though one is peering through a keyhole into a brighter earth long gone, finally enlarging on sheep grazing in a brilliant green meadow, and a little boy in knee breeches and buckle shoes running to an approaching horse and carriage. The simple beauty of those cobblestone streets and the awe-inspiring artistry of those handcrafted

179

homes and furnishings stun with wonder. Believers were actually kneeling down to their God like little children, and all the hope that kissed our country to birth is brought back.

It was as though people still had some innocence then; they were in some way still untouched. George Mason noticed it in the unbelievable defeat of the great British Lion by a handful of tattered farmers. Somehow faith was still running fresh, and the air was clear enough to see a sweeter sun that day when, for the first time on these shores, the Union Jack was hauled down and the Stars and Stripes went up to wave. The glory was not yet too faded for George Mason to tell "that we had been treading on enchanted ground."

In so many ways our world is older and sadder than it once was. The Scioto River beside Sky Farm where I live is now yellow as mud. No one has seen the bottom of it for fifty years. But one old man told me that he had lived along it in the twenties, when it was crystal clear and crammed with perch and trout. His family had lost everything in the Depression. His father had been a trustee of the bank, and they came and took the cattle and finally the farm, and so he and his family had to move into his grandfather's house along the river. They had nothing—nothing except the river. And that was all they needed. The river fed them winter and summer through the Depression. The more they ate, the more fish there were for everyone.

Not anymore. The river is so polluted from industries upstream and the runoff of herbicides from modern farming methods, that only some inedible carp, bony turtles, and a few rock bass remain. Rachel Carson's warning of an approaching *Silent Spring* was not without basis.

I remember that my grandfather's orchards on Sky Farm back in New York were never sprayed, but the favorite Northern Spy apples never had worms. I remember going chestnutting one autumn when I was ten, and my father telling me to enjoy it, for it would be the last time. That year a blight wiped out the chestnut tree in this country. For years afterwards I remember seeing the white skeletons of those dead chestnut trees scattered through midwestern woodlands.

Like the river, the chestnut tree was a secret to the survival of our frontier forebears. One-third of our midwestern woods was chestnut. It never had to be tilled or planted, yet every fall its nuts fattened the pigs and roasted on the hearth, filling the evening with contentment. And chestnut made the best furniture. Even in death the chestnut tree supplied the most beautiful paneling. Some paneling still tries to imitate wormy chestnut. Two-hundred-year-old chestnut beams hewn for old barns are still as strong as ever.

More recently our woodlands have been suffering from the Dutch Elm disease. A few weeks ago there was a depressing telecast of the grave illness which has blighted the majestic Black Forest in Germany, to say nothing of the endangered forests in the U.S.A.

Too much is made of the threat of nuclear holocaust while not enough is said about the acid rains of litter, oil, and tar that have begun to clog our oceans and smog our space, the accumulated residue at the bottom of the wells, and the increasing risk we take every time we draw a breath of what used to be fresh air or take a drink of heavily disinfected water.

Some of us, I am sure, are going to be called to go

upstream and save the river. Just as the youngest can pick up gum wrappers, all of us must fight litter and pollution. Our tradition is filled with those who, like Salk, Edison, and Einstein, have conquered obstacles long considered insurmountable. Every single one of us has some essential part to play in resuscitating earth. Fast.

But we must also be realistic and believe the Gospel. According to the New Testament, earth finally will get out of hand. This sick old world will one day get too old and rotten for us to save by ourselves.

Our armies of soldiers, scientists, and politicians are no match for the fiend, or whatever you call it, that gets into people and kills the wish to live, and makes them murder innocent children because they hate people of another race. Terrorists confess killing not out of courage, but from despair. They actually play Russian roulette. One of them being interviewed recently placed a gun to his head, with one bullet in it, and fired. His friend had gone that way. He will, too.

The New Testament does not believe that the literacy program, or the Peace Corps, or all the aid in the world, will halt this hell-bent perversion that has earth by the throat. We must do all we can, never using our collision course as an excuse; but things are headed for a grand showdown that requires the intervention of God to repair as much as it required Him to invent us.

This concept is so often presented obnoxiously by threatening evangelists, or "I told you so" doomsayers, that many of us have been turned off from believing anything.

Life includes leaving the womb and going away from home. But some believe that is all there is to it, a one-way ticket to our destiny. According to them, "we can never go home again." This secularized evolutionary viewpoint is considered the most enlightened one. Faith in progress is encouraged in school, not faith in some past possibility. Somehow, they say, we will eventually secure enough breakthroughs in surgery and enough self-control.over savagery that we shall evolve into superhumans and make a lasting peace with all our problems.

I find, to the contrary, even more valid reason for turning "back to the future." Grateful for our findings, and mindful of the plagues from which we've been delivered, I honor our homing instinct which leads on to something before—and far more beautiful than—Williamsburg. We ought not to be so preoccupied with endless experiment and restless inquiry that we neglect to appreciate the glorious heights from which we have descended.

Our forebears left us with the belief that we once lived in a Garden in the hand of God, and that the holy and healthy attitude toward life has to do with recovery and restoration of that original blessedness. Everything was once new, and we shall never be able to improve on that. An aging process has been taking place that we want reversed.

Let us, as gracefully as we can, recall our belief in the Second Advent of Christ, which all Christians confess every time we say such words: "And He shall come again in glory to judge the quick and the dead." Jesus did not simply leave us with an example and a Comforter; He left us promising His return.

I realize this presents the most tangled problems and is open to the most absurd speculation. However, if God made us to begin with, and has not left us desolate, then we have faith that He is the Finisher as well as the Author of our faith. In the beginning God saw all that He had made was good. He'll not quit till His ending matches it. We are disillusioned by the utopias and five-year plans and promises of politicians. It is Eden we long for again. Here's the way the Bible ends:

> Then I saw a new heaven and a new earth; for the first heaven and the first earth had passed away, and the sea was no more. And I saw the holy city, new Jerusalem, coming down out of heaven from God, prepared as a bride adorned for her husband; and I heard a loud voice from the throne saying, "Behold, the dwelling of God is with men. He will dwell with them, and they shall be his people, and God himself will be with them; he will wipe away every tear from their eyes, and death shall be no more, neither shall there be mourning nor crying nor pain any more, for the former things have passed away."
>
> Revelation 21:1–4 RSV

The above Scripture refers to a far more successful God than we've generally imagined. Preachers have shrunk heaven's gate into such a needle's eye that it would be of interest only to a very small minority. "The path is narrow that leads to life," does not mean that only a life raft off earth's doomed Titanic will make it. In a way the New Testament is a manual on emergency management. Every one of Jesus' forty parables deals urgently with a matter of life and deadlines. However, all this in no way compromises God's eventual overwhelming triumph over the devil's threat to life on earth.

One well-known sect has insisted for years that only

144,000 souls would be saved. Since their sect now num-
bers many more than that, they are busy revising their
figures. But even if they were to triple those figures, or
enlarge the faithful remnant greatly as most denomina-
tions do, so long as the majority of mankind are not
elected or selected, so long as any lost sheep are dumped,
it reflects against God.

God is not so incapable and Christ so ineffective that
only a fraction of earthlings will make it. Heaven cannot
be built on the graves of billions excluded. Such a calamity
would mean that, so far as most people are concerned,
Jesus is waiting behind the door with an axe. God would
be remembered then, not as the "Father Almighty, Creator
of heaven and earth." He would be remembered either
with horror or embarrassment as the Destroyer. That
burnt-out cinder, earth, would go down in history as the
site of a devastating massacre, no matter how much fun a
handful of saintly survivors might be having on cloud
nine. The last word about earth will not be about the
wretchedness of man but about the overwhelming glory of
God.

We may be losers, but our God is no loser. The New
Testament does not introduce God as a helpless victim of
His children's disobedience. "I believe in God, the Father
Almighty," who drops everything to run and recover a
lost boy, just as one of us would naturally go back to pick
up a mislaid hat. This is the consuming passion of Christ
reflected in His most memorable stories of the lost sheep,
the lost coin, and the lost son, which Luke combines in his
fifteenth chapter.

These unorthodox stories celebrate God's preoccupation
with the lost. Traditionally, God is assumed to be the God

of the good people, chiefly interested in rewarding sheep and punishing goats. No! Jesus' Cross, His great commandment, and these three parables contradict that. God is the God of the loser, the One who goes out of His way for the loser, like a physician in search of the sick. "What man of you, having a hundred sheep, if he lose one of them doth not leave the ninety and nine in the wilderness, and go after that which is lost, until he find it?"

God is not like a bloodhound tracking us down, so we can be policed and punished. God is like a retriever bringing us out of darkness and isolation into the light of His blessed company.

"It is not your Father's will that one of these little ones shall perish." Just like the shepherd, God goes out "If he lose one sheep." We still cannot get a God of statistics out of our heads just as our spiritual forefathers respected "the God of hosts," the God of the army, and we are only beginning to grasp the God of a poor shepherd boy who had to fight a giant. But Jesus develops the concept of a jealous God, like a greedy miser with His own. "Ninety-nine are not enough for God."

God's not simply sentimental about each one, and He's not a quitter; He gets things done. He not only dislikes losing "one," He's determined not to. Charity and compassion are often associated with ineffectiveness: "You win some. You lose some." Not our God. The shepherd, like the woman going through the house for her coin, "searched diligently." Until nightfall? No. Until he was too tired to search further? No. Until he had searched long enough? No. "He searched diligently until he found it." We think we're better at "hide" than God is at "seek." No. Finding is God's obsession.

Luke's stories are not the only scriptural basis for our belief that heaven has no housing problem. Jesus emphasized forgiveness. "If you do not forgive your brother from your heart neither will I forgive you." He featured forgiveness by exaggeration: "Then came Peter to him, and said, Lord, how oft shall my brother sin against me, and I forgive him? till seven times? Jesus saith unto him, I say not unto thee, Until seven times: but, Until seventy times seven" (Matthew 18:21, 22).

Forgiveness is why He came. Forgiveness is the whole idea. He wasn't condoning evil, not anything goes, not the abolition of all penalty. But from the Cross He forgave His killers, obviously revealing a God not to be outdone by the unlimited forgiveness He expects from us. All this makes it hard to see how forgiveness would ever come to an end, how a time would ever come when God would cry, "No more forgiveness. Enough's enough."

Notice also who is special to God; not only one particular person, but the bottom of the list, the least one, the worst one: the nude, the convict, the invalid, the refugee. One gets the impression that when Jesus said, "As often as you did it to one of the least of these, you did it to me," He was reaching for the farthest corners of darkness and despair. Can you imagine Jesus directing us to attend to the farthest tentacles of hell without, as the creed suggests, His own descent into hell?

We do not have a furious God futilely wiping out the bulk of His handiwork in frustration, or to fulfill some abstract notion of justice. We have a "fix-it" God, a God who only reaches His stride in maintenance and repair. He is a photo-finish God, as capable of pulling a losing game out of the fire as He was capable of creating everything out of nothing to begin with. If we are instructed to love our enemies with a love that will never let go, can we ever see the Cross again in any other light than that of a surprisingly athletic Father racing across the fields and leaping fences to reclaim his long lost son in one grand homecoming.

This is not only the epic story of one boy's return. This is the overpowering theme of the Bible. So this is an eschatological story—the story of how it all ends out here in space. With a flying leap in space, our cosmic hero, God, manages to catch this stray bullet, earth.

Haven't you noticed how much responsibility God takes in reaching us. Mary, the teenage peasant girl, was not trying to have a baby, or even praying for a visitation. Gabriel covered all the distance and overwhelmed the completely innocent and unsuspecting girl. She had no part in the birth announcement from above, nothing but praise to God. And the shepherds were not searching for any baby Jesus that holy night. The angels ran across them and sang them in. It was not their earthly pilgrimage, but a celestial expedition that corralled those sleepy shepherds to the stable nearby.

Jesus did not send for John the Baptist to come to His office in Nazareth to baptize Him. Jesus waded out into John's river and cornered him. The first disciples were not on Jesus' back, like office seekers. Jesus caught them fishing. Matthew was doing his taxes when Jesus apprehended him. In one way we wind the Golden String into a ball as we have chosen to walk this way, but Jesus also said, "Ye have not chosen Me. I have chosen you."

Nicodemus took a historic stroll that evening, but it was nothing compared with how far Christ went for him. We do not have a sedentary God waiting sedately for us to report. Jesus made house calls on little girls who were dying, visited healing spas and needy crossroads no one else would think to place on their itinerary. I doubt if that centurion beneath the Cross had put in for the duty in which Christ caught him up.

Now the whole trembling world itself is stretched on a Cross and turns as a thief once did to the One "who for us men and our salvation came down from heaven." And we must never forget that the very first person to believe in the resurrection was a notorious woman of bad reputation. It was not a tribute to her mental accomplishment. It was not the fruition of her struggle of faith. Jesus broke in upon Mary's hysteria as He had done before.

You, too. Wind the Golden String into a ball as best you can. But the best you can do is not good enough. Don't worry, He'll meet you when you can go no farther.

I saw God coming back for us in something that touched my heart long ago. I remember going home from the navy after World War II. Home was so far out in the country that when we went hunting, we had to go toward town. We had moved there for my father's health when I was thirteen. We raised cattle and horses. Some who are born on a farm regard the work and the solitude as a chore, but coming from town, as I did then, made that frugal farm home like Eden to me.

We lived in an old bank house that had been built from bricks made on the place by the first settlers in the Northwestern Territory. (A bank house was one where you could step into the second story from ground level on one side or step into the first story on the lower side.) There was no heat upstairs at all, and I slept in a room with the window-door open all winter in sub-zero weather. I was under about ten blankets and often wakened under a blanket of snow. I got up in the dark at five o'clock and ate breakfasts of saltside and country ham we butchered and seasoned in our own smokehouse.

I realize some of us can look back on our youth and glamorize a life that we actually disliked at the time; but I can honestly say that to me the world of my youth in that isolated wilderness was a place of enchantment. I remember boarding the school bus and smelling skunk coming from some boy whose traps had missed the muskrat. I remember the fever of work at threshing time and those threshing dinners. Women outdoing one another at killing men with pie.

I was entranced when we drove up the mile-long lane to see the old place for the first time—a beautiful example of decaying splendor. The back screen door had a hole in it. When we went inside, there was a pet pig asleep by the fire.

The descendants of the original settlers were still there. They were two maiden ladies who had been teachers till they lost their hearing. One used a hearing trumpet. Her name was Maggie, and she had a heart of gold. Maggie went with the place. She stayed on with my father, mother, sister, and me after we bought the farm. I met her sister, Sarabelle, as I came around the house to the backyard for the first time. It was a cool day in late August, and Sarabelle was making peach butter in a huge black kettle that she stirred with a long wooden hoe to keep her back from the fire.

I started a little flock of Shropshire sheep, the kind that are completely covered by wool except for a black nose and the tips of black legs. My father helped them have their twins at lambing time, and I could tell each one of the flock apart from a distance with no trouble. I had a beautiful ram. A poor man next door had a beautiful dog and a small flock of sheep he wanted to improve with my ram. He asked me if he could borrow the ram; in return he would let me have the choice of the litter from his prize dog.

That is how I got Teddy, a big, black Scottish Shepherd. Teddy was my dog, and he would do anything for me. He waited for me to come home from school, he slept beside me, and when I whistled he ran to me even if he was eating. At night no one would get within half a mile without Teddy's permission. During those long summers in the fields I would only see the family at night, but Teddy was with me all the time. So when I went away to war, I did not know how to leave him. How do you explain to someone who loves you that you are leaving him and will not be chasing woodchucks with him tomorrow as always?

Coming home that first time from the navy was something I can scarcely describe. The last bus stop was fourteen miles from the farm. I got off there that night about eleven o'clock and walked the rest of the way home. It was two or three in the morning before I was within half a mile of the house. It was pitch dark, but I knew every step of the way. Suddenly Teddy heard me and began his warning barking. Then I whistled only once. The barking stopped. There was a yelp of recognition, and I knew that a big black form was hurtling toward me in the darkness. Almost immediately he was there in my arms. To this day, that is the best way I can explain what I mean by coming home.

What comes home to me now is the eloquence with which that unforgettable memory speaks to me of God. If my dog, without any explanation, would love me and run to take me back after all that time, would not my God?

Hang on to your Golden String and keep going as long as you can, but also watch for His approach. He is also coming for you. Heaven's gate built in Jerusalem's wall is not stationary. Like my dog story, and the story of Jesus' Father, Heaven is mobile and already on its way to you. "And I saw the holy city, new Jerusalem, coming down out of heaven from God, prepared as a bride adorned for her husband" (Revelation 21:2 RSV).

Bring me my bow of burning gold!
Bring me my arrows of desire!
Bring me my spear! O clouds unfold!
Bring me my chariot of fire!
William Blake
"Jerusalem"